Organizational Conflict

Managing Organizational Conflict

Sam Blank

McFarland & Company, Inc., Publishers
Jefferson, North Carolina

This book has undergone peer review.

LIBRARY OF CONGRESS CATALOGUING-IN-PUBLICATION DATA

Names: Blank, Sam, 1947– author.
Title: Managing organizational conflict / Sam Blank.
Description: Jefferson, North Carolina : McFarland & Company, Inc., Publishers, 2020. | Includes bibliographical references and index.
Identifiers: LCCN 2019047015 | ISBN 9781476678924 (paperback) ∞
 ISBN 9781476637907 (ebook)
Subjects: LCSH: Conflict management. | Communication in management. | Organizational change.
Classification: LCC HD42 .B583 2020 | DDC 658.4/053—dc23
LC record available at https://lccn.loc.gov/2019047015

BRITISH LIBRARY CATALOGUING DATA ARE AVAILABLE

ISBN (print) 978-1-4766-7892-4
ISBN (ebook) 978-1-4766-3790-7

© 2020 Sam Blank. All rights reserved

No part of this book may be reproduced or transmitted in any form or by any means, electronic or mechanical, including photocopying or recording, or by any information storage and retrieval system, without permission in writing from the publisher.

Front cover illustration © 2020 Shutterstock

Printed in the United States of America

McFarland & Company, Inc., Publishers
Box 611, Jefferson, North Carolina 28640
www.mcfarlandpub.com

For tremendous love and support of all kinds,
I thank my wife Ellen Afromsky,
my brother Ralph, and my children
Leah and Matthew

Acknowledgments

In writing this book, I have many people to thank. I would like to thank my colleagues and good friends who encouraged me along the way and who have shared with me their experiences and taught me meaningful lessons: David Avdul, Alan Borer, Richard Bradley, Jennifer Brady-Cotter, Tzu-Wen Cheng, David W. Fuchs, Eva Kolbusz-Kijne, Susana Powell, Ellen Raider, Kerry Ruff, Maria Volpe, and Norman Wechsler.

I appreciate and am grateful to the mentors that have shaped me to be the person I am today: Constance Bernardi, DeWitt Clinton High School; Thomas Bloch, Stuttgart, Germany; Joseph A. DeVito, Hunter College; William E. Hug, Teachers College, Columbia University; Michael Pritchard, Heartland Media; and Sandra Sollod Poster, Borough of Manhattan Community College.

Special acknowledgments must go to my students who over the past years have provided the inspiration essential to this kind of task. I am indebted to my cadre of stellar communication studies students at the Borough of Manhattan Community College of the City University of New York: Ryan Bias, Jennifer Cachola, Andrea Cano, Nechama Gluck, Anne Goren, Margarita Khodzka, Maria Camila Martinez, Daniel Murphy, Juliette Perez, Iva Porfirova, Elizabeth Shin, Anastasia Sidorenkova, and Natasha Sokorina.

Thanks are due as well to my colleagues at the American Management Association whose valuable input was always welcomed and to my colleagues at the New York City Department of Education, Office of the Manhattan Superintendent who collaborated with me in the administration of the District Conflict Resolution Centers initiative and the District School Leadership Team.

Table of Contents

ACKNOWLEDGMENTS vi
PREFACE. 1
INTRODUCTION. 5

1. Aspects and Causes of Conflict in an Organization
Interests, Identities and Attitudes 9
Organizational Learning 10
Characteristics of a Learning Organization 12
Learning Ground Rules 14
Problem-Based Learning 15
Team Learning 16
Organizational Conflict 17
Work Group Role Expectations 20
Organizational Personality Dimensions 21
Organizational Development 23
Organizational Behavior 24
Interpersonal and Intrapersonal Conflict 27
Aspects of Trust in Conflict 28
Cultural Differences and Conflict 30
Gender Influences 31
Ambient Cultural Disharmony 32
Cross-Cultural Leadership 33

2. Conflict: Unavoidable Aspect of Organizational Life
Major Trends 35
Conflict Areas 36
Anticipating Conflict 39
People Issues 40
Employee Assessments and Social Exchange Theory 40

Sources of Conflict ....
Working Behaviors ....
Language and Styles of Conflict ....
The Cost of Organizational Conflict ....
Hidden Costs ....
Gearing Up for Training and Development 47
Leading Change 49
Redefining Leadership 51
Resistance to Change 52
Employee Resistance Is Challenging 53

3. Transformational Organizations
Why Organizations Fail 55
Transformational Leadership and Organizations 58
Leadership and Manager Differences 60
Exemplary Leadership 61
Differences Among Workers, Managers and Leaders .. 63
Organizational Measurement 63
Workplace Communication 64
Workplace Channels and Networks 68
Power and Influence 71
Personal Attributes as Leverage 74
Types of Leverage 75
Sharing Power in Organizations 76
Power and Politics 78
Managing Change and Stress 81
Implementing Dynamic Change 87
Using the Johari Window at the Workplace 91

4. Ethical, Moral and Human Issues in Organizational Conflict
Guidelines, Principles, Codes 94
Ethical Leadership 96
Values Conflict 98
Intellectual Capital 99
Conflict Management Styles 100
Individual Profile Styles 102
Motivations 103
Managing Differences 105
Group Thinking 107
Generational Differences 110
A New Mindset 113

Reaction to Crises and Catastrophes 114
Workplace Violence. 117
Crisis Prevention and Management 119
Crisis Management Team 120
Organization's Crisis Plan 121

5. Workplace Collaborations
Advantages of Collaboration 123
Group Purpose 125
Types of Collaborative Groups 126
Successful Groups 127
Collaborating and Not Competing 128
Functional and Dysfunctional Team Collaborations 130
Poor Collaboration 131
Positive Collaborative Efforts. 134
Collaborating to Get More. 135
Collaboration and Achievement. 136
Virtual Teams 137
Six Thinking Hats. 139

6. Conflict Resolution Approaches
Strategies, Purposes, Practices 143
The Flowchart of Conflict 145
Conflict Resolution Techniques 145
Negotiation 146
Receive and Then Deliver 148
Three Basic Negotiation Strategies 148
Competitive and Cooperative Negotiation. 149
A True Negotiation Situation? 150
Team Negotiation. 153
Framing in Negotiation. 155
Questioning in Negotiation 157
Listening in Negotiation 158
Listening and Seeking to Understand Content and Feelings 161
Nonverbal Listening 162
Negotiation and Ethics 163
Smart Negotiators. 165
Negotiation Obstacles and Deal Killers. 166
What About Mediation? 167
Third-Party Assistance/Arbitration 172
Types of Arbitration Used by Organizations 174

7. Confrontational Innovation and Design

Common Design Thinking Tenets..............................175
Engagement and Confrontation................................176
Types of Dissent...177
Difficult Conversations......................................178
Competencies to Handle Confrontation........................180
Unmanageable Levels of Confrontation........................181
Turbulent Times in a Company................................183
Dismissal and Termination...................................184
Preparation for Taking Action...............................185
Management of Opportunities.................................186
Assertive Confrontation.....................................187

8. Conflict Management

Approaching Employee Conflict...............................189
Openness of the Manager.....................................191
Management Productivity.....................................191
Conflict Manager Focus......................................193
Two Messages..194
Manager's Toolbox...195
Playing Fair..195
Taking Charge...196
Managers and Critical Thinking..............................197
Managers as Change Agents...................................200
Influencing the Future......................................201
Dynamic Network Theory......................................202
Imperatives for Effective Managers..........................204

Case Studies

Case Study 1—Noisy Neighbors................................207
Case Study 2—Apple Bashing..................................208
Case Study 3—We Deliver.....................................209
Case Study 4—Working in HR..................................209
Case Study 5—The Team Project...............................210
Case Study 6—New Boss, New Rules............................211
Case Study 7—You're Under Arrest............................211
Case Study 8—The Melt—Hops and Wine Stop—Taki-Slow..........212
Case Study 9—Hawaii Beachwear Project.......................212
Case Study 10—Oh, What a Feeling............................213

References..215

Index..221

Preface

This is a book about positive conflict resolution strategies that stimulate innovation and growth where companies can look to synergistic solutions to common issues and needs. It examines the dysfunctional outcomes of organizational conflicts that result in job stress, reduced communication between individuals and groups, and the fostering of a climate of distrust, where working relationships are damaged and job performance is reduced.

The current matrix structure that has been adopted by many companies has resulted in increased competition for resources, unclear reporting lines, and general confusion and varying management styles. A strong need exists to examine the basic tenets of conflict, organizational behavior and conflict management that are vital to the overall success of the organization.

The book is apportioned to address five objectives that are targeted to (1) aid organizations and individuals to recognize and accept conflict, whether internal or external; (2) examine and successfully manage the unavoidable aspect of conflict in organizational life; (3) view the organizational process within ethical, moral and human issues and act in a conflict prevention mode, rather than an intervention mode; (4) foster a company culture that uses conflict resolution approaches that incorporate proactive confrontational innovation and design; and (5) reexamine and provide a new model for the role of the company conflict management.

The concepts presented in this book were fashioned after spending more than 25 years as a mediation and negotiation trainer and teaching at the Graduate School of Educational Leadership of Pace University and the City University of New York. In my professional career, I have found that it is not only necessary to provide learners with concrete knowledge, but it is also essential to challenge them to use and adapt the materials to fit into their own lives and connections. I had a desire to author a book in organizational conflict that would accompany and complement my consultative work with business executives, administrators and management personnel. It is central that readers view the contents of this book within the overall picture of the many complexities of changing organizational structures and environments.

There are very few books on the market today that address the prevalent occurrence of organizational conflict, and, in fact, this area only received cursory mention in human relations textbooks and organizational behavior and design texts. The field of conflict and crisis management is certainly supported by a very long history of research, yet there are only three titles I found available that address conflict in organizations.

They are *Managing Conflicts in Organizations* by M. Afzalur Rahim, published by Routledge in 2010; *Crisis in Organization* by Laurence Barton, published by South-Western in 2001; and *Hostage at the Table: How Leaders Can Overcome Conflict, Influence Others, and Raise Performance* by George Kohlrieser, published by Jossey-Bass, 2006.

This book is written in an informative and conversational style which includes many opportunities to examine and practice conflict resolution in ten case studies and engage in stimulating role plays. This book has added sections on areas of leadership and organization development, active listening and communication, managing generational differences, and fostering collaborations. It offers insights for company professionals who are tasked with managerial decisions and problem-solving. All the material was created and designed to assist organizations to meet conflict head-on and bring issues to resolution.

In the United States, over a decade ago, employees spent close to three hours per week dealing with conflict and 25 percent of employees avoided conflict by calling in sick or being absent from work. Most of the U.S. workforce have never received conflict management training. There is a special aptitude needed to successfully work disputes through to resolution, and this book can help leaders improve their connection and interaction skills by applying solid conflict management strategies and tactics.

The material is written for many different groups. The primary audiences for this book are employees, executives, business owners, managers, team leaders, and human resource personnel. Studying and pursuing a focus in conflict resolution, organizational behavior, negotiation, crisis management, and change management will improve communication and increase productivity. A secondary market for this book is the undergraduate and graduate college student studying business management, crisis intervention and prevention, organizational and industrial psychology, and team and leadership development.

Designing, implementing, communicating, using and modifying an organizational conflict management system will require constant feedback and reinvention. Organizational conflict management policies can be the determining factor in the success or failure of the conflict management system and the eventual success of a company. Businesses that see conflict resolution as a vital program to managing organizational conflict demonstrate that collaboration is the best approach to resolving disputes and continuing to build trusting relationships.

Companies are driven to be profitable and employees engaged in arguing and criticizing others do not help the company bottom line. Conflict management goes a long way in strengthening the bond among the employees where they can feel motivated at work. Conflict management and conflict resolution also play an important role in our personal lives. At a time when our world is undergoing changes and the economy is not stable, organizations must embrace all the tools at their disposal to minimize and resolve internal and external conflicts to remain vibrant and profitable. While advancement in negotiating, mediating and resolving conflicts has been considerable, there is still a compelling need to deal with disputes and workforce differences in improved and healthier ways.

Introduction

Conflict is omnipresent, and if one wanted to put money into a growth industry, this would be an area to invest in! Organizations large and small move forward and measure successes by examining the bottom line—profit. Most businesses focus on daily operations and develop short-term and long-term strategies and benchmarks. These objectives and missions and contingency plans will take a back seat when conflict arises that impacts workers, stakeholders, company morale and industry image.

In 1982, Johnson & Johnson's Tylenol medication commanded 35 percent of the U.S. over-the-counter analgesic market, representing something like 15 percent of the company's profits. Unfortunately, at that point, one individual succeeded in lacing the drug with cyanide. Seven people died as a result, a widespread panic ensued about how widespread the contamination might be, and by the end of the episode, everyone knew that Tylenol was associated with the scare. The company's market value fell dramatically. While this problem was not a result of conflict within the organization, Johnson & Johnson needed to bring resolution to the problem and re-bolster its corporate image. They decided the product would not be re-established on the shelves until something had been done to provide better product protection. As a result, Johnson & Johnson developed the tamperproof packaging that would make it much more difficult for a similar incident to occur in the future.

Within five months of the disaster, the company had recovered 70 percent of its market share for the drug, and the fact this went on to improve over time showed that the company had succeeded in preserving the long-term value of the brand and their conflict management effort addressed their public image.

On April 17, 2018, the treatment of two black customers by a Starbucks manager in Philadelphia and their resulting arrest brought this large organization into conflict/crisis mode. Exactly what transpired between the two men and the manager who asked them to leave and then called police is unclear. However, the outcome is clear. Two black customers were treated in a way markedly different from what most people experience with the Seattle-based coffee giant. Its stores are intentionally designed as public gathering spaces, and most visitors take advantage of them, and the restrooms, without incident. Starbucks has repeatedly demonstrated, by its longstanding corporate focus on social responsibility and inclusion, that this singular conflict in one brick and mortar facility could have a drastic effect on the entire company. Starbucks CEO Kevin Johnson promptly apologized, took personal responsibility and met with the men. The company also took the extraordinary step of scheduling the closure of 8,000 company-owned stores in the U.S. on the afternoon of May 29 for training to prevent discrimination. That doesn't make what happened right, but the company's response is a useful model for other businesses and individuals when confronting a conflict situation that impacts its brand and public image.

The study of organizational behavior examines attitudes and performance within the company setting, which draws on the theories and methods on principles from psychology, sociology, cultural anthropology and individual and group behavior (Ivancevich, 2002). Various organizations have different goals, interests and priorities beyond profit. However, when a conflict arises within a company, the overriding and mitigating factors to a successful resolution lie in figuring out what differences led to the conflict, what personality and leverage issues exist, what communication pitfalls may have exacerbated the conflict and what appropriate problem-solving techniques can be applied.

The chapters in this book have been designed to help profit-based organizations, government organizations, non-profit organizations, and individuals recognize conflict, whether internal or external. The approach to examining and managing conflict is to provide comprehensive information about organization design and behavior, power and influence, interpersonal, intrapersonal and intragroup conflict. The management of and reorientation to differences, leadership and team structures as well as reactions to crisis and catastrophes are also addressed. This book will help change an organization's way of thinking about conflict and will foster a company culture that is based upon principles of agreement and resolution. In a time when executives, managers, human resource and training personnel, and employees must do more with fewer resources, this book will assist with increased productivity and improve human communication among all individuals. In his 2002 article in *The International Journal of Conflict Management* author M. Afzalur Rahim indicated that (1) there is no clear set of rules to suggest when conflict ought to be maintained at a certain level, when reduced, when ignored, and when enhanced; (2) there is no clear set of guidelines to suggest how conflict can be reduced, ignored, or enhanced to increase organizational learning and effectiveness; and (3) there is no clear set of rules to indicate how conflict involving different situations can be managed effectively.

Many organizations use professional specialists to establish clear guidelines and to work on conflict and dispute issues. These individuals are often part of a human resources department and the conflict issues, major and minor, and the resolutions do not fully address the "totality" of a workplace conflict. It may be deemed successful if the conflict issues don't escalate. These are organizational reactive responses and they may not address underlying issues of the emotional and social issues of the workforce. There is a clear need for organizations to use conflict resolution specialists, with superb competencies, to address, manage, and resolve conflict issues.

Conflict refers to more than just overt behavior. Concentrating only upon its behavioral manifestation is extremely limiting. The very focus of the concept of conflict emphasizes the need to (1) consider the situation in which parties (individuals, groups or organizations) come to possess incompatible goals; (2) analyze their structure of interaction; and (3) examine the nature of their goals. It is also important to consider emotional and cognitive orientations that accompany a conflict situation.

As we attempt to understand conflict in organizations the world around us is changing and years after Rahim's article, not much has changed or improved. Indeed, some managers and organization leaders have taken positive steps to identify, research and resolve conflicts. Organization leadership must meet conflict straight on regarding the company's mission, direction, and design, so that things can be accomplished while working most effectively with people (Fullan, 1991).

1

Aspects and Causes of Conflict in an Organization

Interests, Identities and Attitudes

Conflict can be viewed as many things. Schellenberg (1996) defined social conflict as "the opposition between individuals and groups on the basis of competing interests, different identities and/or differing attitudes." The three vital elements of this definition highlight the sources of difference—interests, identities and attitudes. These take varying shapes in different organizations. The interests of the IT department can be very different than those of the accounting department. The identities of the managerial vice-presidents will differ from those of project managers, and the attitudes of the CEO, COO and CFO will be different from those of the administrative assistants in the organization.

Since conflict is inevitable and all organizations will have to deal with the varying issues surrounding conflict, it is noted that many researchers and text materials point out that conflict is not always bad. The reframing of conflict as a problem or crisis can result in viewing conflict as an opportunity to think creatively and to work collaboratively on resolutions and agreements. The Chinese symbol for crisis clearly indicates the reframing modes: the peril and danger and a way of thinking about a crisis as an opportunity to look at a situation with new eyes, a chance for improvement and change, and lessons to be learned.

Conflict can be an important vehicle through which the work of an organization gets done. In some cases, conflict enhances the adoption of new policies and procedures and assists in maintaining the stability of the organization. Reaching resolutions and agreements to organizational conflicts may fall to the disputing parties, employees and their supervisors, human resource departments, peer review committees, or specialized conflict resolvers or negotiators. In their landmark book *Getting to Yes: Negotiating Agreement Without Giving In*, Ury, Fisher and Patton (2011) describe three dilemmas facing conflict resolvers: (1) soft negotiators offering quick concessions to reach amicable agreements; (2) hard negotiators viewing conflicts as a battle to be won; and (3) principled negotiators deciding issues on their merits and looking for mutual gains.

The authors, describing the straightforward method of principled negotiation, break it down into four basic points:

People—Separate the people from the problem.
Interests—Focus on interests, not positions.
Options—Invent multiple options looking for mutual gains before deciding what to do.
Criteria—Insist that the results be based on some objective standard.

Organizational Learning

Organizational learning involves a continuous process that enhances its collective ability to accept, make sense of, and respond to internal and external change. Organizational learning is more than the sum of the information held by employees. It requires systematic integration and collective interpretation of new knowledge that leads to collective action and involves risk taking as experimentation.

Peter Senge (2006) described learning organizations as places "where people continually expand their capacity to create the results they truly desire, where new and expansive patterns of thinking are nurtured, where collective aspiration is set free, and where people are continually learning how to learn together."

Learning organizations (Gavin, 1993) are skilled at five main activities: systematic problem solving, experimentation with new approaches, learning from their own experience and history, learning from the experiences and best practices of others, and transferring knowledge quickly and efficiently throughout the organization.

One of the most valuable lessons in learning is that there is always something new to learn. Finding new solutions and high-quality alternatives to solutions depends on an organization's climate. When stakeholders are involved in training, learning sessions, company fact-finding retreats and periodic team building and brainstorming sessions, the organization benefits in many ways. These type of "learning sessions" need not focus solely on team skills or enhancing social relations. Learning is the way we create new knowledge and improve ourselves. Although there is ample debate regarding the mechanisms and scope of learning, in its simplest form this is no different for organizations.

In November of 2010 the Starbucks Corporation and Kraft Foods Inc. began airing a messy divorce in public, fighting over the dissolution of their partnership selling bags of Starbucks coffee at supermarkets.

News of the breakup first surfaced when Starbucks Chief Executive Howard Schultz said on a quarterly conference call that Starbucks wanted to end its 12-year deal with Kraft, which markets and distributes Starbucks and Seattle's Best coffees to supermarkets and stores like Target. Kraft also sells Starbucks discs for its Tassimo one-cup coffee brewer and Tazo teas. Kraft Foods initiated arbitration to challenge Starbucks' attempt to end the agreement.

It contended that if Starbucks wanted to back out, it must pay Kraft the fair market value of the business plus a premium of as much as 35 percent. Under the deal with Kraft, Starbucks bagged coffee sales grew to $500 million (U.S.) a year from $50 million. Additionally, Starbucks shares were down 2.8 percent in morning trade, while Kraft shares were down 1.4 percent. Starbucks could end up paying more than $1 billion if it were forced to compensate Kraft for the business.

Starbucks was willing to risk the potential cost of a dissolution as it sought significant growth beyond its cafe chain by looking to the market for packaged consumer goods. The company was also pushing sales of its Via instant coffee in what it hoped would become a billion-dollar business.

After holding team information and learning sessions Starbucks informed Reuters it planned to work with the sales and marketing division of privately held Acosta Inc, which handled its Via business, to distribute Starbucks coffee to stores after ending its ties to Kraft on March 1, 2011.

This business dispute illustrates how fluid marketplace trends can be, which can cause negotiated business agreements to become undesirable over time. In their original agreement, Kraft and Starbucks would have been wise to agree upon set times for renegotiation. They would have had leeway to revisit existing deal terms in the face of changed economic and industry conditions. They could also have negotiated conditions for ending the agreement early, such as cancellation penalties and other forms of compensation. This could have been worked out as both companies conducted updated learning sessions. Intelligent and continual learning can help anticipate uncertainties which have the potential for a costly business dispute. In the end, on November 12, 2013, an arbitrator ruled that Starbucks should pay $2.23 billion in damages plus $527 million in pre-judgment interest and attorneys' fees to Kraft Foods. This ruling put an end to the years-long battle between Kraft Foods and Starbucks.

Learning from this costly experience, Starbucks has grown to rely heavily on organizational learning and development opportunities which is evidenced by:

- company growth by an average of two stores per day for the last 27 years;
- an ambitious plan to add 1,000 stores in China;
- a corporate plan to spend more on employee healthcare than coffee beans;
- the fact that its stock is worth over 23 times what it sold for in 1992; and
- classroom learning opportunities and training, which include self-guided booklets and "learning coaches."

Characteristics of a Learning Organization

Too often, training and learning programs in organizations are conducted because competitors are doing it, because an executive believes that conducting a certain program would be a good thing to do, or because some crisis demanded new learning approaches and strategies. Learning organizations can always make use of additional and updated training. Training can help organization members to learn and develop. However, training targeted at supporting and enhancing organization change can have considerable payoff (Burke, 2011).

Learning organizations facilitate the active learning of their employees so that the organization can continuously transform itself. A learning organization inspires to employ a more interconnected way of thinking. Active learning and training modules combine actual problem-solving in organizations with "learning about how to work together better, how to solve organizational problems more efficiently and effectively, and how to improve the learning process in general—learning about learning." One of the main benefits of becoming a learning organization is the company's ability to adapt to changing situations.

To assess learning status of organizations, use the scale of numbers below to rank the following eight statements:

1 (Highly Important)
2 (Important)
3 (Negligibly Important)
4 (Not Important)
5 (Definitely Not Important)

___ The organization has a clear and orderly learning and instructional program.
___ The organization uses many methods to keep in touch with how the workforce feels about their training programs.
___ The organization sets high standards for worker achievement and does not let inferior work get by.
___ The organization management admits its shortcomings and errors about poor, or lack of, training opportunities.
___ The organization allows the workforce to have input and make decisions about future learning opportunities.
___ The organization keeps up to date on available learning, technology, and industry trainings.
___ The organization places great emphasis on the employees learning to work together effectively and to understand one another.

After the rankings have been made, individuals should form into small groups and discuss the various sections so as to arrive at consensus about the importance of the items as they relate to professional standards of learning and competence.

In an article in the *New York Times* (Casselman, 2018), a story appears of how a company in Hicksville, Ohio, dealt with a conflict involving slow productivity growth. APT Manufacturing, which builds and installs robotic equipment to help other manufacturers automate their assembly line, received requests for more robots to help their labor crunch. The conflict for APT Manufacturing was that the organization faced a hiring challenge because "the pool of skilled workers is shallow." Rather than turn to robots himself, Anthony Nighswander, the president of ATP Manufacturing, made a low-tech decision involving learning and training opportunities. The organization began offering apprenticeships, covering the cost of college for its workers, and, three years ago, started teaching manufacturing skills to high school students in their own facilities.

sponsibility for their own learning. This learning and the acquisition of new knowledge will help to cultivate better communication and interpersonal skills that support conflict resolution and negotiation issues.

Researchers on the facilitation of PBL have identified general issues connected with infusing this seamlessly in the structure of an organization (Savin-Baden, 2003). Three components are (1) support that is constructive and empowering; (2) direction that involves encouragement and respects individual autonomy; and (3) structure that is stable and relatively predictable.

Three modes of PBL facilitation are (1) hierarchical, in which facilitators take a controlling and directive role by setting objectives; (2) cooperative, involving a sharing of power with the team in order to enable them to be self-directed learners; and (3) autonomous, fully respected with a facilitator simply setting the conditions in which the learning will take place (Heron, 1993).

In an organizational context, PBL

- is learner-centered;
- is composed of small groups, usually 10–15 participants;
- uses facilitators to guide learners rather than instruct;
- identifies a specific problem to serve as the focus of the group and stimulates learning;
- uses a problem as a vehicle for the development of problem-solving skills, thereby stimulating the cognitive processes;
- has learners work on a development problem; and
- is a method to organize the learning of both the organization's matrix and models to incorporate the newest trends impacting the company's business practices, products and/or services.

Team Learning

Organizations are much more likely to perform well when employees work effectively as a team. Good teamwork creates synergy, where the combined effect of the team is greater than the sum of individual efforts. Synergy is the interaction or cooperation of two or more organizations, substances, or other agents to produce a combined effect greater than the sum of their separate effects.

Whether learning teams are small or large, it is crucial to structure team learning into an organization's larger training program. Providing collaborative activities over a long period of time will allow employees to assume responsibility for their own learning, create strong and positive bonds among employees, and decrease the likelihood of conflicts that could develop and, perhaps, grow into crisis situations for both a work team as well as the entire organization.

One of the ways to initially structure and involve employees in team learning is to form study groups or teams to analyze work or learning materials and then explain it to one another. Another way is to form group inquiry teams to receive work-related materials and share and discuss items they do not fully comprehend. This sharing can create team cohesion. A third way is to utilize flipflop learning, where members of a team are given different materials and are requested to study them and teach them to one another.

As work and the working context become increasingly complex and ambiguous, teams and individual team members must be able to learn and adapt. This includes learning how to work together as a team. To promote team learning (Silberman, 2006) and make optimum use of time, some questions to consider would include the following:

1. How were teams composed (random assignment, diversity, homogeneity, prior acquaintance, work-related assignment)?
2. Were the team invited to establish ground rules for discussion and function?
3. Did the teams receive less structure as they obtained competencies and indicated they could assume more control over their own learning?

Teams become high-learning teams when they implement four practices. First, a climate for learning must be established. Second, the team's work must be assessed. Third, the organization may assign a leader to the team. Lastly, the teams should be capable of managing knowledge (Lindoerfer, 2008).

Organizational Conflict

The causes of organizational conflict fall into two distinct categories. The structural aspects of conflict arise mainly because of the issues related to the design of the organization as well as its sub-divisions. One of the important considerations relates to the relative size of the organization. The larger the size of the organization, the greater the basis for existence of conflict. It is likely that as the organization becomes larger, there will be greater impersonal formality. With many supervisory levels, supervision may become diluted or distorted. All of these factors can propagate conflict.

The behavioral aspects of conflict arise out of human thoughts and feelings, emotions and attitudes, values and perceptions, and they reflect some basic traits of a personality. Conflict can also arise due to differing viewpoints about various issues. For example, highly hierarchical organizations and supervisors might antagonize workers by highlighting differences, causing the workers to overreact and causing a conflict.

Classical organization theory evolved during the first half of this century. It represents the merger of scientific management, bureaucratic theory, and administrative theory. Max Weber (1947) stressed the need to reduce diversity and ambiguity in organizations and his focus was on establishing clear lines of authority and control. His bureaucratic theory emphasized the need for a hierarchical structure of power. It recognized the importance of division of labor and specialization. A formal set of rules was bound into the hierarchy structure to insure stability and uniformity. Weber also put forth the notion that organizational behavior is a network of human interactions, where all behavior could be understood by looking at cause and effect.

Conflict in the organization as viewed through the lens of classical management theory was rigid and mechanistic. The shortcomings of this theory quickly became apparent. Its major deficiency was that it attempted to explain people's motivation to work strictly as a function of economic reward and made no provisions for conflict resolution theory.

Many organizations that reacted negatively to classical organization theory looked to a human relations movement theory that displayed a genuine concern for human needs and the desire to resolve conflicts amicably.

Barnard (1968) proposed one of the first modern theories of organization by defining organization as "a system of consciously coordinated activities." He stressed the role of the executive in creating an atmosphere where there is a coherence between values and purpose. Organizational success was linked to the ability of a manager to create a cohesive environment. He proposed that a manager's authority is derived from subordinates' acceptance, instead of the hierarchical power structure of the organization.

People don't stop being people at work. Conflict, unfortunately, is inevitable. However, organizational conflict theory states that there are several varieties of conflicts within an organization, interpersonal being only one type. Divisions and departments have conflicts with one another, senior managers have power struggles and organizations even have conflict with other organizations. But there is not a consensus on what it all means. Some theorists say conflict must be resolved, others say that it drives success (Feigenbaum, 2008). Feigenbaum goes on to postulate his "maturity and immaturity theory."

One theory holds that people in their career lives want to grow and mature with increasing levels of responsibility and opportunity, just as they do in their personal lives. However, many hierarchical organizations, for the sake of efficiency, break jobs into specialties, giving employees narrow scopes and duties, which they are expected to perform well. As a result, employees don't get to use all their talents and abilities and feel constrained and unable to develop. The result is conflict between employees and the organization itself. On individual levels, workers may develop resentment and apathy and, in some circumstances, sentiments can take on larger dimensions and employees can begin to formally or informally organize, sometimes forming unions. Organizations that promote a high degree of specialization and little mobility may find themselves with higher turnover because of the conflict stemming from this maturity-immaturity theory.

Tensions in organizations can also be a result of intergroup conflict. This can occur because of the roles and functions of teams and departments (Belak, 1998). Intergroup relations between two or more groups and their respective members are often necessary to complete the work required to operate a business.

Many times, groups interrelate to accomplish the organization's goals and objectives, and conflict can happen. Some conflict, called functional conflict, is considered positive, because it enhances performance and identifies weaknesses. Dysfunctional conflict, however, is confrontation or interaction between groups that harms the organization or hinders the attainment of goals or objectives.

The consequences of intergroup conflict may result in members who overlook individual differences uniting against the other side. The group can become more efficient and effective at what they do, and members can become more loyal, closely following group norms. Problems can occur, however, when the group loses focus of the organization's goals and becomes closed off from other groups.

In other circumstances this type of conflict can be healthy. An example would be two accounting teams that compete to devise new methods of forecasting growth for the best results. While there may be some issues between them, they drive each other to perform better, producing better systems for more accurately forecasting and determining best practices for projecting higher profits for the company.

Organizational Conflict

INTERPERSONAL   INTRAGROUP   INTERGROUP   INTERORGANIZATIONAL

Work Group Role Expectations

Roles are aligned with a set of opportunities for the successful functioning of a work undertaking. Role conflict is a stressor that can occur in the workplace when personal values conflict with job responsibilities. Roles may be poorly defined and incompatible roles may be performed. In some cases, role conflict happens when there are contradictions between different roles that a person takes on or plays in their work life.

Functional work group roles can include both task and maintenance roles. To successfully and productively attain these goals, team members must take responsibility for identifying and performing the functions, either task or maintenance based, required by the team at any given moment. Generally, task functions keep groups headed toward decisions and actions. Maintenance functions help build a group's sense of identity and develop the social relationships in a work group.

Maintenance roles facilitate communication and resolve conflicts. Individuals who perform these roles are often involved in monitoring and gatekeeping the emotional state of the work group, supporting and encouraging other team members, and helping to relieve tension and anxiety within the group. These individuals are the social-emotional leaders and team harmonizers. Individuals who exhibit the maintenance role help to bring out opinions and feelings and are quick to dole out recognition. They offer or accept compromises and will usually admit errors to help build trust and cohesion in the work group. An important expectation of the maintenance role is to encourage silent members to participate and assist in suggesting procedures for communication that keeps the group on task while promoting equal power.

Task roles refer to the actions of individuals that help move the project, decision, and work task along. They are the individuals who spearhead the achievement of the task. They are actively involved with initiating and defining the problems and suggest procedures and solutions to give the work team direction. They also solicit facts and clarification that enable the group to collect relevant data. Task roles assist in defining and interpreting ideas, issues and alternatives to help eliminate confusion.

The third type of role individuals adopt is that of a hindrance nature. Employees in work groups often present problems and are the impetus for conflicts. Their disruptive nature may take the shape of dominating, which may include taking much meeting time expressing their own self-centered views and opinions. They may attempt to remove themselves from discussions or decision-making and/or refuse to participate or cooperate with group decisions. Group work conflicts can arise if they discount, disregard, or minimize group or individual ideas.

The digressing individual rambles, tells stories, and takes the group away from its primary purpose. This hindrance employee may also be negativistic and stubbornly resist, disagree and oppose teammates without or beyond "reason" and attempt to maintain or bring back an issue after the group has rejected or bypassed it.

Organizational Personality Dimensions

Conflict within a company involves the workforce at many levels. Individuals' interests, identities and attitudes, discussed at the beginning of this chapter, are involved in the initiation of conflict, the escalation or de-escalation of the conflict and the success or failure of a resolution. The Myers-Briggs Type Indicator (MBTI) is an introspective self-report questionnaire with the purpose of indicating differing psychological preferences in how people perceive the world around them and make decisions.

The MBTI was constructed by Katharine Briggs and her daughter Isabel Briggs Myers (1943). It is based on the conceptual theory proposed by Carl Gustav Jung, who speculated that humans experience the world using four principal psychological functions: sensation, intuition, feeling, and thinking. The dimensions defined by the MBTI are as follows.

- Extroversion-introversion—the degree to which people differ with respect to sociability and being energized while around

others, as compared with introversion, which stresses keeping more to oneself.
- Intuition-sensing—the degree to which people depend more on intuitiveness for embracing information, as compared with a penchant for fact-based data—that is, more of a function of one's individual senses.
- Thinking-feeling—the degree to which people differ with respect to what they do with data once they absorb it, as compared to a preference to rely more on emotional considerations when making decisions.
- Judging-perceiving—the degree to which people prefer planning, achieving closure and decisiveness, rather than keeping options open and being spontaneous.

Research indicates that leaders of high performing organizations endeavor to shape and maintain an optimally-balanced workforce culture. To accomplish this is to push aside the tendency for company leaders or managers to shape the culture toward one or two patterns at the expense of others which can add to an unbalanced organizational culture. Some of the cultural patterns in organization (Truskie, 2010) which tend to map the Meyers-Briggs functional pairings are:

(1) cooperative pattern which is based on the team concept and includes the positive elements of cooperation, team work, sharing, diversity, and collaborative problem solving; (2) inspiration pattern which emphasizes the importance of treating people as individuals who desire meaning in their employment and in their lives. Positive elements include job challenge, engagement, recognition, career planning, and training and development which enhance worker motivation and inspiration; (3) achievement pattern [which] places importance on the need to achieve excellent organizational performance and includes positive elements of discovery, innovation, competition, being the best, and striving for excellence; and (4) consistent pattern which emphasizes the need for discipline throughout the organization to obtain consistent results. The positive elements include order, rules, standardization, planning, follow-through, and measurement. Each culture pattern is valuable, and brings its own merits to the organization, but overusing one at the expense of the others can inhibit growth for the organization.

Defining a problem that involves an organizational personality dimension is the very first step in attempting to resolve the problem. Deriving a solution is not tantamount to visualizing what the actual problem is. For example:

> A department supervisor has called an emergency meeting with her direct reports ten minutes before the end of the workday and states, "We have a problem with our team project and someone will need to work three hours overtime tonight!"

This cooperative pattern, based on team concept and sharing, is not the problem, because the supervisor offered the solution (a team member will need to work overtime). As we have seen, shaping and maintaining balance in a work team is important for success and for the organization to mature and flourish.

Organizational Development

The long-range effort to improve an organization's problem-solving capabilities and its ability to cope with changes in its external environment is what organizational development is about. A classic definition of organization development comes from Richard Beckhard's (1969) *Organization Development: Strategies and Models*. "Organization development is an effort that is planned, organization-wide, managed from the top, increases organization effectiveness and health, and incorporates planned interventions in the organization's processes, using behavioral-science knowledge."

It is not a surprise that the unit of analysis for OD practitioners in organizations focuses on developing organization capability through alignment of strategy, structure, management processes, people, and rewards and metrics. Some people get confused about the differences between organizational development departments and human resources departments.

Human resources professionals are primarily concerned with the efficient management of the employment process (from recruitment to termination). HR also focuses on helping the organization comply with governmental regulations and on mitigating employment-related risks.

Human resources are concerned with

- managing the hiring, retention, and performance processes;
- mitigating employment-related risks;
- ensuring legal compliance;
- confirming there is "enough" equity and diversity;
- enforcing policies and procedures;
- reducing labor costs; and
- promoting workplace health and safety.

Organizational development, on the other hand, was created as a way of applying behavioral science to help organizations improve individuals and systems. OD's goal is to help people function better within an organizational context. At its heart, OD is supposed to represent purposeful and meaningful change for the better.

Effective organizational development seeks to improve effectiveness while adhering to the organization's culture and values. Success in this area maximizes employees' potential and helps them amplify their contributions in furtherance of the organization's success. It also can assist in aligning human behavior with the organization's strategy, processes, and business objectives.

Successful OD efforts require skilled behavioral scientist interventions, a system view and top-level management support and involvement. British Airways, the second largest airline in the UK, was created in 1974 from four other companies: BEA, BOAC, Northeast Airlines, and Cambrian Airlines. It operated with 215 aircraft supported by 50,000 employees, a level of staffing that was, even then, viewed as precariously oversized. The oil crises of the 1970s shrank the airline's customer base, and its huge staff resulted in massive financial losses. The company soon developed a reputation for terrible service as a result.

In 1981, British Airways brought on a new chairperson, Lord King, who noticed that the company was operating very inefficiently and wasting valuable resources. To increase profits, King decided to restructure the entire organization by reducing its workforce from 59,000 to 39,000, eliminating unprofitable routes, and modernizing the fleet. He repaired the airline's image by bringing in a new marketing expert. Within 10 years, the airline reported the highest profits in its industry: $284 million.

Before King began announcing layoffs, he explained his reasons for the restructuring to the entire company to prepare them for the upcoming change. Without his transparency, British Airways could have experienced employee backlash and negative press around all the layoffs. But he always communicated honestly and frequently to manage the change.

Organizational Behavior

Organizational behavior (OB) is a field of study that investigates the impact that individuals, groups and structures have on behavior within an organization to enable applying this knowledge toward improving organizational effectiveness. Organizational behavior is an important concept for any organization, since it deals with the three determinants of behavior in organizations: individuals, groups and structure.

Organizational behavior then applies the knowledge gained about individuals, groups and the effect of structure on behavior to make organization's work more effectively. OB is concerned with the study of what people do in an organization and how their behavior affects the organization's performance. Because OB is concerned with employee related situations, it tends to emphasize behavior related to work, absenteeism, employment turnover, human performance and management. The organization's base rests on management's philosophy, values, vision and goals.

The purpose of organizational behavior is to gain a greater understanding of those factors that influence individual and group dynamics in an organizational setting so that individuals and the groups and organizations to which they belong may become more efficient and effective. The field also includes the analysis of organizational factors that may have an influence upon individual and group behavior. This speaks directly to conflict, conflict management and conflict resolution.

As a relatively new, interdisciplinary field of study which draws most heavily from the psychological and sociological sciences, it also looks to other scientific fields of study for insights. One of the main reasons for this interdisciplinary approach is because the field of organizational behavior involves multiple levels of analysis, which are necessary to understand behavior within organizations because people do not act in isolation—that is, workers influence their environment and are also influenced by their environment. This in turn drives the organizational culture which is composed of the formal organization, informal organization, and the social environment.

OB is an applied science, and as Terri Scandure writes, the four goals of science are (1) description (examining what the process looks like); (2) prediction (as to whether the process will occur again); (3) explanation (as to why the phenomenon is happening); and (4) control (of whether the change will happen) (Scandura, 2019).

Scandura provides the following example:

> The forecasting of extra workers needed for a toy store during the holiday season is an important process for ensuring the best customer service. HR understands how many customers will visit the store based upon prior holiday seasons. The store managers have an understanding why customers visit the store and when volume increases.

Prediction is important since managers need to project with accuracy how many additional workers they will need to hire to meet customer demand. However, hiring forecasts aren't always accurate. In this example, the science is moderate for prediction. For control, one could say the science is low because there are many reasons why customers may not visit the store that are outside of the organization's control. The better the initial understanding of how many workers will be needed, the better the store manager should be able to predict how many seasonal workers to hire and for how long.

One of the principled applications of OB is targeted toward the improvement of stakeholders' skills. Developing these skills, especially for supervisors and managers, helps an organization to attract and keep high-performing employees. Incorporating OB principles can help transform a workplace from good to great with a positive impact on the bottom line. Because OB is concerned with employment-related situations, it examines behavior in the context of job satisfaction, absenteeism, employment turnover, productivity, human performance, and management [Robbins and Judge, 2018].

The introduction of new products in an organization requires multiple levels of analysis before the innovations and changes take effect. Organizational behavior aimed at improving effectiveness must provide clear insights to all stakeholders. Tesla, Inc., founded in 2003, is an American multinational corporation based in Palo Alto, California, that specializes in electric vehicles, lithium-ion battery energy storage and solar panels. In the last week of June 2018, Tesla reported that they had reached a manufacturing milestone, producing more than 5,000 Model 3 sedans in a week. The company will need to prove that it's not a one-time achievement. The organizational behavior model at Tesla is counting on the Model 3, its first mass-market vehicle, to increase revenue and offset the billions of dollars it has been spending to establish a battery plant in Nevada. CEO Elon Musk stated that it established new solutions, which were thought impossible, to turn a profit in 2018's final two quarters. Changes in personnel, although not in the original behavior model, helped the organization overcome bottlenecks and glitches in their Model 3 assembly process.

However, Wall Street, especially banking and securities firm Goldman Sachs, was not impressed by Tesla's Model 3 milestone and the stock plunged 7 percent on negative notes regarding a brake test report. Goldman Sachs noted that Model 3 reservations declined to 420,000 from 455,000 last year. The company fell short on its second-quarter deliveries by posting 40,740 vehicles delivered versus the Wall Street consensus expectation of approximately 51,000.

Interpersonal and Intrapersonal Conflict

Interpersonal conflict is an important concept. Here is one possible definition of interpersonal conflict.

> *An interpersonal conflict is a disagreement between two individuals or subgroups of an organization involving significant resentment and discontent. This suggests that not all disagreements are interpersonal conflicts. Due to differences in values and beliefs, there may be many interpersonal disagreements.*

Conflict resolution or conflict management strategies could involve finding ways to reduce feelings of resentment and discontent. For example, helping people to see things from the other person's perspective may help to resolve conflicts by reducing resentment. People may more clearly see the validity of certain arguments, or critically evaluate their own views.

Lewicki, Barry, and Saunders (2016), writing in *Essentials of Negotiation*, report that conflict results from an opposition or disagreement. It arises when there is an interdependence, between people or your own thoughts, and the goals that need to be achieved cannot both happen.

In interpersonal conflict one experiences conflict with other individuals. This is a major level of conflict and can occur between coworkers, siblings, spouses, roommates and neighbors. This is the form of conflict most people have in mind when they think about being in conflict.

According to Lewicki, Barry, and Saunders, intrapersonal conflict is also called intrapsychic conflict. It occurs within the individual. This conflict can develop out of one's own thoughts, ideas, emotions, values and predispositions. Intrapersonal conflict occurs when people internally argue with themselves about something, such as when they want a new pair of sunglasses, but they know they shouldn't spend the money.

These types of conflicts are encountered daily and one must negotiate them. One may think of conflict as negative, but both interpersonal and intrapersonal conflict can have benefits. Healthy conflict provides one with the skills to develop better relationships, gain an understanding of oneself, increase one's resolution skills and avoid negative and damaging reactions. Intrapersonal conflict can be disruptive and stressful if we do not understand our own needs and desires.

Organizations are a whole entity with interacting components. We have seen that individuals, teams, groups, departments and divisions all confront conflict, chaos and crisis in differing manners. Multiple perspectives of the causes of conflicts and the paths to resolution give us keen insights to how successful organizations move forward to improve the internal company structure and find new directions. Methodologies for dealing with change and conflict are unique to each organization.

Yet today with the consistency of change surrounding us "one might argue that all organizations, to ensure long-term survival, effectiveness, and success, should be attempting to change in the same direction, that is, to be nimble, flexible and adaptable; in short, to be changed so that the norm, the culture is one that constantly is in a state of change" (Burke, 2011).

Interpersonal and intrapersonal conflicts that are manifested in organizations, when addressed with a sense of purpose and urgency, can lead to dramatic change. Several commonalities of the successful process of organizational change (O'Toole, 1995) that can be married to positive conflict resolution are (1) the changes had top-down management support; (2) the changes were built on the unique strengths and values of the organization; (3) specifics of the change were not imposed from the top; (4) the change was holistic, with open system theory; and (4) the changes were approached from a stakeholder viewpoint.

Too often there is much talk about ongoing change and conflicts in organizations, with little real action. We know more today about intrinsic motivations, conflicts involving interests and needs, and the importance of communication and listening skills. One of the most important factors in maximizing the excellence of a group's product was the degree to which the members were able to create a state of internal harmony, which allowed them to take advantage of their full talents (Goleman, 1995).

Aspects of Trust in Conflict

At the very core of all human relationships is the dynamic of *trust*. With trust, business deals get done; without it, they are vulnerable to changing incentives and circumstances. An imbalance of power can corrupt a business climate; so does a violation of trust. Trust is the belief that another individual or company is benevolent and honest. People gain the trust of others when they see others perform cooperative actions and reciprocate in trusting ways (Cahn & Abigail, 2014).

It is very hard to know what motivates a negotiation or business adversary. Are they willing to cooperate with you to meet both your interests or just to serve theirs? Trust with a counterpart must be built so that interests can align and increase the likelihood of a successful agreement. A powerful way to establish trust is to employ one of the mind's most basic mechanisms for determining loyalty: the perception of similarity. If we can make someone feel a link with us, their empathy for and willingness to cooperate with us will increase. Success is increasingly dependent on developing cooperative ventures and developing more creative business solutions. All business ventures, opportunities and negotiations involve risk. Deepening the trust of trust minimizes this risk.

Trust is right at the foundation of the survival and success of any business. Without trust, there can be no sustainable business, and it is a strategically critical issue in any type of relationship. Over the long term, business success is dependent upon a network of positive relationships. In these relationships the four benchmarks that need to be assessed (Beamer and Varner, 2008) are verifiability, trustworthiness, accuracy, and credibility.

As a company HR manager, how would you respond to Theresa in the following scenario?

....

Theresa Trustworthy

Theresa Root indicated to the Vegan Soup Company that she would begin as a full-time "flavor" consultant next week, at an agreed upon salary. The project will begin in one week.

She called HR at Vegan Soup stating that her current company is willing to offer her $3,800 more and a bump in her position at the company in the future to remain. Would you be willing to match this request? What issues involving trustworthiness, credibility, and loyalty exist? Considering Theresa's talents, are there other factors that come into play when contemplating a decision?

....

Trust in almost all conflicts is crucial. All parties involved in a conflict resolution situation need to trust that the established process will help them achieve agreements. A large study of group dynamics discusses the types of social support that underlie trust in the workplace (Forsyth, 1999).

Emotional support	Rewarding and encouraging others Listening to problems and shared feelings
Informational support	Giving ideas, advice and suggestions Explaining how tasks can be performed
Task support	Helping with work tasks Providing supportive actions
Belonging	Expressing approval and acceptance Demonstrating belonging to the group

Cultural Differences and Conflict

In 1997, Nike released the "Air Bakin," a basketball sneaker that featured a generic, flame-like design. They also featured this design in their "Air BBQ" and "Air Grill." Unfortunately, when viewed from right to left, the flames resembled the Arabic word for Allah when written in Arabic script.

Soon after its launch, the Council on American Islamic Relations (CAIR) released statements condemning this product. After Nike made a failed attempt to conceal the emblem by covering it with a fabric patch and red paint, CAIR's president threatened a boycott against Nike products worldwide. Nike eventually recalled 38,000 pairs of the shoe, apologized to the Muslim community, and built playgrounds for Islamic youth organizations in Falls Church, Virginia, and other communities.

In a globalized economy, cultural sensitivity is essential. Understanding and knowing about cultural differences is a crucial skill for success. Understanding language nuances, etiquette and cultural time management differences can assist in the navigation of complex interactions. Minimizing miscommunication between people and companies from different cultures is a daunting challenge. Unintentional missteps can ruin costly international marketing efforts.

The study of cultural orientation can provide people with models for understanding and predicting the results of intercultural encounters. Different cultures arrive at truth in different ways that include faith, facts, and feelings. To explore these, as well as to derive and understanding of different cultures, different backgrounds, different business practices and protocols, I recommend *Kiss, Bow or Shake Hands: The Bestselling Guide to Doing Business in More Than 60 Countries* (Morrison and Conaway, 2006).

Globalization is exposing most countries to interactions and relationships with people, products and services, yet many organizations are not prepared for this global and highly competitive arena. Companies doing business in foreign countries may view cultural differences as a giant, extraordinary, and complex issue guiding the actions and responses of humans in every walk of life. They must give attention to everything people do to survive and advance in the world. Cultural programs will not work if critical steps are omitted or if people unconsciously apply their own rules to another system. Organizational communication, in the global marketplace, has more to do with sending the right response than sending the *right* messages (Hall and Hall, 1990).

Gender Influences

Assertive, confident, and dominant are just some of the characteristics associated with leadership, yet when we think of employees that have those traits, we generally tend to think of males. The reasoning is years of hardwiring from a biological history of women playing the role of nurturing caregiver. How does gender bias really affect women in the workplace?

Gender affects conflict dynamics at the societal and individual level. Understanding the role of gender in conflict is best accomplished through an analysis of three different levels: individual, interactional and societal.

Gender also affects dispute handling mechanisms. In *Gendered Lives: Communication, Gender and Culture*, Julia T. Wood (2010) postulates that the processes used to resolve disputes for women were less effective than for men. For example, women were more often transferred laterally instead of resolving the dispute. According to work by gender expert Dr. Deborah Kolb (2015) of the Simmons School of Management, men are more apt to withdraw from a conflict situation than women.

In the same book, *Negotiating at Work: Turn Small Wins into Big Gains*, Kolb and coauthor Jessica L. Porter write that women often are the "peacemakers" in their organizations. The women they studied acted as informal peacemakers within their organizations. The women got involved in people's conflicts because coworkers sought them out. They provided a sympathetic ear to their coworkers. They also became involved because they were loyal to the organization but also cared how the organization treated people. They provided support for people to tell their story, they reframed people's understandings of the situation, they translated people's perceptions of each other, and they orchestrated occasions for private conflicts to be made public. Women in the study were ambivalent about their role and skills as peacemakers within the organization. They felt that the important roles they filled in the organization were not understood or appreciated.

Deborah Kolb's earlier work focused on how women's ways of understanding the world based upon essential differences affected their conduct in negotiations. Kolb focused on four themes that define women's place in negotiations: (1) a relational view of others; (2) a contextual and related definition of self and situation; (3) an understanding of control through empowerment; and (4) problem solving through dialogue. Women's voices are different because of early social development and women's places in negotiation are different because of structural systems of discrimination.

Carol Watson (1996) examined whether gender or power was a better predictor of managers' negotiation behavior. She hypothesized that perceived gender differences in negotiation behavior are an artifact of status and power differences between men and women. This study provides a more realistic review of the legitimacy of such gender stereotypes by comparing the effects of power and gender on negotiator behavior.

Ambient Cultural Disharmony

Harvard Business School Assistant Professor Roy Y. J. Chua (2013) started asking questions about "hostile work environment" that occurred in cases of sexual harassment or racial discrimination where coworkers' morale or performance suffered even when they were not the direct targets of abuse. He coined a term for the phenomenon: "ambient cultural disharmony."

Awareness of our own cultural biases and assumptions can go a long way toward improving creativity in multicultural situations. Managers could decrease the effects of ambient cultural disharmony by encouraging employees to identify their own assumptions of other cultures. An example is keeping a cultural journal in which they record their thoughts and observations. Managers can create cultural "awareness moments" by setting up site visits between employees working in different environments, or by encouraging them to work side by side to observe how cultural differences can influence work habits.

Remarkably, while ambient cultural disharmony can decrease creativity, ambient cultural harmony may not promote creativity. That reflects human nature, Chua says. "As human beings, we pay more attention to negative information because it is a signal of danger. Positive information tends to be given less weight."

Managing cultural friction in this way might not only help create a more harmonious workplace overall, but also ensure that companies are reaping the creative benefits of multiculturalism at its best. Interestingly, while ambient cultural disharmony decreased creativity, ambient cultural *harmony*—that is, observers experiencing people from other cultures having a good relationship—did not promote creativity.

Cultural awareness is not necessarily a skill per se. A skill is more about the ability to do something well or very well. Being culturally aware is a lot simpler than it sounds. Organizational cultural awareness is about being aware that as people from different cultures, we can and will sometimes look at the same thing in different ways. Organizations need to be open to the fact that we are not all the same, or meant to be the same, and that when working with people from different cultures, we may sometimes need to check the assumptions we are making and the conclusions we are drawing about others' intentions and behaviors.

Cultural awareness is not something that can only be achieved through a learning/training course. Within business and commerce, being culturally aware means one tries to understand how cultures can differ in their approaches to areas such as building trust, communication, meetings, pitches, management, sales, and negotiating.

Cross-Cultural Leadership

Cross-cultural leadership is needed in diverse markets with a multicultural workforce. This leadership can attract and retain top talent that can increase profitability and cost saving. The goal of leading with cultural intelligence (Livermore, 2015) is to build relationships, determine goals, and build agreement. Organization leaders must be cognizant that different cultures view help in the building of agreement in innumerable ways. Some look at these as "bottom up" strategies, while others incorporate "top down" thinking.

Our places of employment are often the most diverse settings in our lives. Relationships with coworkers tend to cut across race, gender, religion, sexual orientation, and political persuasion. Because of this, workplace environments have the potential to make us better at working across differences. Yet, as businesses often represent a microcosm of society, many companies find it difficult to avoid the animosity that society's divisiveness creates. Some studies show that workplace tension causes both generalized stress and an increased reticence in regard to talking about controversial issues, even when they impact the work.

When left unaddressed, the increasing tribalism that's segregating our society can spill into and undermine work environments. Forward thinking companies need to take up the important work of addressing issues of diversity, culture, and finding common ground to avoid conflicts and the escalation of workplace tension.

2

Conflict: Unavoidable Aspect of Organizational Life

Major Trends

We can all conclude that conflict is an unavoidable aspect of organizational life and that it is a natural phenomenon. Wherever individuals of different backgrounds congregate, whether in the workplace, groups or associations, conflict is bound to occur. The growth of conflict may depend upon many factors that include constant change, greater employee diversity, more work teams (virtual and self-managed), less face-to-face communication (more electronic interactions), and a global economy with increased cross-cultural dealings.

Organizations have entered a new era characterized by rapid, dramatic and turbulent changes. The accelerated pace of change has transformed how work is performed by employees in diverse organizations. Change has truly become an inherent and integral part of organizational life and conflict will always be an unavoidable aspect.

A comprehensive review of conflict literature yielded this consensus definition: "conflict is a process in which one party perceives that its interests are being opposed or negatively affected by another party." In another sense, conflict may be viewed as a state of open, often prolonged fighting: a battle or war. Another definition describes it as a state of disharmony between incompatible or antithetical persons, ideas, or interests who are interdependent. A simplistic description defines conflict as a disagreement through which the parties involved perceive a threat to their needs, interests or concerns.

With a disagreement, there is usually some level of difference in the positions of the two (or more) parties involved in the conflict. But the true disagreement versus the perceived disagreement may be quite different.

In fact, conflict tends to be accompanied by significant levels of misunderstanding that exaggerate the perceived disagreement considerably. If we can understand the true areas of disagreement, this will assist us in solving the correct problems and managing the true needs of the parties. This perceived disagreement reflects the ways we regard conflict. We can choose to deal with it, avoid it, or resolve it.

The parties of the company that are involved often see disparities in the sense of who is involved in the conflict. Sometimes, employees are surprised to learn they are a party to a conflict, while other times they are surprised to learn they are not included in the disagreement.

People respond to a perceived threat at work, rather than the true threat, facing them. Thus, while perception doesn't become reality, often people's behaviors, feelings and ongoing responses become modified by that evolving sense of the threat they confront. If we can work to understand the true threat (issues) and develop strategies (solutions) that manage it (agreement), we are acting constructively to manage the conflict.

There may be a tendency to narrowly define "the problem" as one of substance or task. However, workplace conflicts tend to be far more complex than that, for they involve ongoing relationships with complex, emotional components. There are always procedural needs and psychological needs to be addressed within the conflict in addition to the substantive needs.

Conflict is a problematic situation where (1) the conflicting parties are interdependent; (2) they have the perception that they seek incompatible goals or outcomes or they favor incompatible means to the same ends; (3) the perceived incompatibility has the potential to adversely affect the relationship if not addressed; and (4) there is a sense of urgency about the need to resolve the difference.

Conflict Areas

In the broad range of conflicts, there are four distinct general areas. Interpersonal relationships usually include those between siblings, partners and friends, but can also include coworkers, employees and supervisors, and neighbors. A second important category of conflicts is those that occur in groups or teams. This may include families, work project teams, classes and clubs. Conflicts in this arena have been studied extensively and offer a large range of conflict situations for analysis (Folger, Poole, Stutman, 2013).

A third important arena for conflict is the organization. Organizations often see conflicts arise over issues of struggles for promotion, differences over project funding, and issues over strategic directions. Transcending most organizational conflicts is the notion that one or more of the four classified types of issues are present.

- *Interpersonal conflict* refers to a conflict between two or more individuals. This occurs typically due to how people are different from one another. We have varied personalities which usually results in incompatible choices and opinions. Apparently, it is a natural occurrence which can eventually help in personal growth or developing your relationships with others.
- *Intrapersonal conflict* occurs within an individual. The experience takes place in the person's mind. Hence, it is a type of conflict that is psychological, involving the individual's thoughts, values, principles and emotions. Intrapersonal conflict may come in different scales, from the simpler, mundane ones like deciding whether to wear brown or black shoes to work, to ones that can affect major decisions such as choosing a vocational path. This type of conflict can be quite difficult to handle if you find it hard to decipher your inner struggles. It can lead to restlessness and uneasiness and can often affect the way you contribute to and work on a team project.
- *Intragroup conflict* is a type of conflict that happens among individuals within a team. The incompatibilities and misunderstandings among these individuals lead to an intragroup conflict. It may arise from interpersonal disagreements (e.g., team members have different personalities which may lead to tension) or differences in views and ideas. Within a team, conflict can be helpful in coming up with decisions which will eventually allow them to reach their objectives as a team. However, if the degree of conflict disrupts harmony among the members, then some serious guidance from a different party will be needed for it to be settled.
- *Intergroup conflict* takes place when a misunderstanding arises among different teams within an organization. For instance, the sales department of an organization can come in conflict

with the public relations department. This is due to the varied sets of goals and interests of these different groups. In addition, competition also contributes to intergroup conflicts.

The struggle to prevent and contain company conflicts requires that the workforce's basic human needs are met. These are not concepts that are broached by a prospective employee at a job interview. Job descriptions, salaries, status, working conditions and benefits are important to an employee. The four classifications of issues above do not enter into interview questions or concerns.

The sources of conflict can come from many corners. Glencore, a Switzerland-based mining and commodities trading company, found itself involved in a money-laundering and corruption investigation that had connections to the Democratic Republic of Congo, Nigeria, and Venezuela. The intragroup conflict occurred when individuals at Glencore made materially misleading disclosures. Although Glencore was not charged with a crime, this conflicting issue sent its company's share price down as much as 13 percent (Reed, 2018).

In Robert Bacal's (1998) book on conflict prevention, the author states that there are three ways of looking at organizational conflict. Each of these ways is linked to a different set of assumptions about the purpose and function of organizations.

The Bad—dysfunctional view of organizational conflict is imbedded in the notion that organizations are created to achieve goals by creating structures that perfectly define job responsibilities, authorities, and other job functions. Like a clockwork watch, each "cog" knows where it fits, knows what it must do and knows how it relates to other parts. This traditional view of organizations values orderliness, stability and the repression of any conflict that occurs. This view causes problems.

The Good—functional view of organizational conflict sees conflict as a productive force, one that can stimulate members of the organization to increase their knowledge and skills and their contribution to organizational innovation and productivity. Unlike the position mentioned above, this more modern approach considers that the keys to organizational success lie not in structure, clarity and orderliness, but in creativity, responsiveness and adaptability.

The Ugly—we have the good (conflict is positive), the bad (conflict is to be avoided), and now we need to address the ugly. Ugly occurs where the manager (and perhaps employees) attempts to eliminate or suppress conflict in situations where it is impossible to do so. When ugly occurs in organizations, there is a tendency to look to the leader/manager as being responsible for the mess. In fact, that is how most employees would look at the situation. Management and employees must work together in a cooperative way to reduce the ugliness and increase the likelihood that conflict can be channeled into an effective force for change.

Fulfilling a worker's basic needs can prevent and reduce conflict. Abraham Maslow's (1954) studies on human needs can have specific connections to the workplace in the following ways:

> **Psychological**: The work environment should be comfortable.
> **Safety and security**: Employees should not have to worry about their personal safety.
> **Social**: Organizations with a history of social and other camaraderie-building activities usually have a higher degree of employee engagement that creates an atmosphere of belonging.
> **Esteem**: Employees want to sense that they are being challenged and achieving. They desire to feel that their contributions matter and will be recognized.
> **Self-actualization**: Self-actualization in the workplace translates to maximizing one's true potential and contributes to one's personal and professional development and career growth. Employees can feel trusted and empowered.

In the realm of the workplace, the more an organization can do to assist its employees to find relevance, value and meaning in their work, the more it will treasure the highly motivated employees and the reduction in conflict.

Anticipating Conflict

What are the keys and signs for organizational managers to observe so that they can anticipate and perhaps head off situations that produce functional or dysfunctional conflicts? Alan C. Filley (1975) listed several antecedents of conflict. Some of these include (1) incompatible personalities or value systems; (2) overlapping or unclear job boundaries; (3) competition for limited resources; (4) organizational complexities; (5) unreasonable or unclear policies, rules, or standards; and (6) unmet expectations as well as unresolved or suppressed conflicts.

Many of these antecedents of conflict are a potential minefield for managers or team leaders. Personality conflicts, intergroup conflicts and, in some cases in which companies deal with other cultures, cross-cultural conflicts can pose a threat to the successful functioning of the organization. By adopting a process view of conflict, we can see that conflict is dynamic, ongoing and not static.

At Hong Kong's Lingnan University, Dean Tjosvold (1993) noted that the three desired cooperative conflict outcomes within organizations are focused on (1) agreements that are equitable and fair; (2) stronger relationships which build bridges of goodwill and trust for the future; and (3) learning that promotes greater self-awareness and creative problem-solving.

People Issues

William Schneider (2017) has identified several issues individuals have at the workplace that could lead to potential conflicts.

Distrust	Low level of accountability
Low morale	Reluctance to raise concerns
Workflow bottlenecks	Frequent leadership changes
Confusion about responsibility	Overworked people
Turf battles	Passing the buck

Employee Assessments and Social Exchange Theory

Organizations that seek competitive advantages through employees should be able to manage the behavior and results of the entire workforce. The formal performance appraisal review system was viewed as the primary source for managing work performance. Some supervisors and managers may dislike confrontation and conflict and expend as little time as possible giving employees feedback. In the interest of providing regular feedback, performance reviews should not be an annual event. Many progressive companies conduct quarterly meetings with employees and others meet twice a year.

No matter the components of a performance review process, some have argued that these appraisal systems are imperfect and inconsistent because they are autocratic and manipulative. The importance of performance reviews is to establish employee goals, document a job plan and expectations, and communicate performance strengths and weaknesses. The primary purpose of appraising employees is to instill in them the desire for continuous improvement. Yet the outcome of many performance appraisals is frequently a decrease rather than an increase in performance. Among the reasons for this decrease is the belief by employees they are being evaluated for the wrong things, by the wrong manager. Employees' emotional anguish grows when the person who is evaluating them lacks objectivity and appears not to be fair (Latham, Almost, Mann and Moore, 2005).

Social exchange theory proposes that people evaluate the costs and rewards of a relationship by the amount of effort required to attain rewards and avoid costs (West and Turner, 2000). People in relationships, groups and organizations often ask, "What does this relationship have to offer me?" From this social exchange theory, conflict arises when one individual believes that the outcomes are too low and perceives that the other person may resist any attempt to raise outcomes. For example, one spouse may see constant fighting and high tension as too much of a cost to personal happiness and decide to opt for a divorce.

Many encounters at work are made up of a certain amount of give and take, but this does not indicate that the give and take are always equal. Social exchange suggests that it is the valuing of the benefits and costs of each relationship that determine whether we choose to continue a social association. At the workplace, divorce is an unlikely option.

Social exchange theory suggests that we essentially take the benefits and subtract the costs to determine how much a relationship is worth. Positive relationships are those in which the benefits outweigh the costs while negative relationships occur when the costs are greater than the benefits. Because conflict is an inevitable part of day-to-day life in organizations, its management is a very important factor to consider for the well-being of an organization. When the balance is deemed as incorrect, not fair, or askew, conflict can result, and if not addressed, can fester, grow and become toxic to the organization.

Sources of Conflict

Taking a closer look at what causes conflict can help us understand this phenomenon even more. What are the factors that make conflict arise? Three main sources of conflict as proposed by American psychologist Daniel Katz (1978) are economic, value, and power.

Economic conflict is brought about by a limited amount of resources. The groups or individuals involved then come into conflict to attain the most of these resources, thus bringing forth hostile behaviors among those involved.

Value conflict is concerned with the varied preferences and ideologies that people have as their principles. Conflicts driven by this factor are demonstrated in wars wherein separate parties have sets of beliefs that they assert (in an aggressive manner, at that).

Power conflict occurs when the parties involved intend to maximize what influence they have in the social setting. Such a situation can happen among individuals, groups or even nations. In other types of conflict, power is also evident as it involves an asserting of influence on another.

Conflict comes naturally; the clashing of thoughts and ideas is a part of the human experience. It is true that it can be destructive if left uncontrolled. However, it does not have to be something that can only cause negative things to transpire. It is a way to come up with more meaningful realizations that can certainly be helpful to the individuals involved. Positive outcomes are reached through an effective implementation of solid conflict resolution initiatives. Effective conflict managers see opportunities to resolve differences and improve relations among employees.

Working Behaviors

Accurate communications, high levels of trust and rational thinking build working relationships that are, hopefully, conflict free. Difficult workplace behaviors can inhibit performance in others and will only deteriorate if left alone, contaminating more people and incurring hidden costs for the organization. It takes many forms like rudeness, yelling, shunning, mobbing, gossiping, refusing to talk to or acknowledge others, harassing, incessant complaining to supervisors, ignoring directives, and slow working (Belak, 1998).

Most conflicts within and involving people revolve around unfulfilled needs, primarily the psychological need for control, recognition, affection, and respect. At its simplest level, the behavior manifested in the rejection of a workmate creates obstacles to problem-solving. Our behaviors at work must include a willingness to deal with our work partners as *real* persons (Fisher and Brown, 1988). Possessing unfulfilled needs is common but when it is displayed as problematic, it must be addressed.

There is no quick and easy answer, but there is a signal and direction to *change* the behavior in others. It takes time and patience to cure such negative characteristics, and it doesn't help to ignore the problem behavior. Professional conduct is to be expected at the workplace and organizations can find strength in diversity. Different people have different perspectives on issues, and that can be valuable for solving problems or generating new ideas. Being unable to understand why someone holds a viewpoint doesn't mean that they're wrong.

Language and Styles of Conflict

We can agree that conflict is inevitable, and many see conflict as a growth industry, but these conflict issues need not get out of hand and result in project management failures or job demotion or job loss. Everyday language certainly reflects the variety of ways we regard conflict. We can talk about handling conflict, dealing with it, avoiding it or resolving it (Cahn and Abigail, 2014). Many organizations invest time, money and personnel to engage in conflict management. People resources and human resources divisions are often tasked with designing, coordinating and administering "peer review committees" to deal with conflicts. Another concept is conflict resolution which relies on disputes to reconcile their issues, wants and needs so that order can prevail and the organization is not negatively impacted. Both approaches are entrenched in effective communication, active listening and a melding of common interests and outcomes.

Understanding the language of conflict means to be able to state primary and secondary conflict issues, priority issues, the development of an array of creative solutions and resolutions and forging a mutually acceptable agreement. Three language of conflict workplace metaphors are conflict as opportunity: "What are all of the creative opportunities for resolving this issue?"; conflict as a journey: "Let's work extremely hard to seek common ground"; and conflict as a battle: "We were able to shoot down that idea."

Seeing increased contention in the world, Christopher Moore (1996) was one of the first to assert a strong need for people and organizations to have more information on how conflict occurs, what the barriers are to resolution, and what specific actions could be taken to address the conflicts. He noted that conflict is caused by a variety of differences, each pointing to five different types of conflict—data, interest, relationship, value, and structure.

Data conflicts are caused by a lack of information or misinformation, different views on what is relevant, different interpretations of data, and different assessments of procedures. Interest conflicts are caused by a perception of actual competition, procedural and psychological interests. Relationship conflicts develop because of powerful and robust emotions, stereotypes, poor communication or miscommunication, and repetitive negative behavior. Value conflicts are caused by the different criteria for evaluating ideas, exclusive intrinsically valuable goals, and different ways of life or ideology. Structural conflicts are caused by destructive patterns of behavior or interaction, unequal control, ownership, distribution of resources, power and authority, and time constraints.

In the early 1970s, two grad students, Ralph Kilmann and Kenneth Thomas (1974), developed a new way of assessing how individuals processed and achieved conflict resolution. They determined that existing ways of testing an individual's habitual mode of resolving conflict put an unrealistic emphasis on "collaboration" as the best solution. They reassessed the data and came up with a new way of assessing how individuals handle conflict that countered the tendency of test-takers to choose "collaboration" *because it's perceived as the socially most desirable resolution method.* Their findings were published academically, and the Thomas-Kilmann Instrument (TKI) became a short test that determined individual conflict resolution profiles. The TKI quickly found wide acceptance. While Kilmann and Thomas developed the concept of five ways of resolving conflict, Robert Blake and Jane Moulton (1964) had identified five conflict resolution modes and published their results a decade earlier. The TKI helps individuals identify the one or two dominant modes they are the most comfortable using for most conflict situations.

1. *Avoid (I Lose, You Lose)*—This is when you avoid or side-step the issue or withdraw from the conflict situation. You aren't helping the other party reach their goals, and you aren't assertively pursuing your own. This works when the issue is trivial or when you have no chance of winning. It can also be effective when the issue would be very costly. It's also very effective when the atmosphere is emotionally charged and you need to create some space.
2. *Accommodate (I Lose, You Win)*—This is when you cooperate to a high degree, and it may be at your own expense and work against your own goals, objectives and desired outcomes. This approach is effective when the other party is the expert or has

a better solution. It can also be effective for preserving future relations with the other party.
3. *Compromise (We Both Win, We Both Lose)*—This is the "lose-lose" scenario where neither party really achieves what they want. This requires a moderate level of assertiveness and cooperation. It may be appropriate for scenarios where you need a temporary solution or where both sides have equally important goals. When you compromise, each side concedes some of their issues to win others. This style is most useful when you look to bring a conflict to quick closure.
4. *Compete (I Win, You Lose)*—This is the "win-lose" approach. You act in a very assertive way to achieve your goals, without seeking to cooperate with the other party, and it may be at the expense of the other party. This approach may be appropriate for emergencies when time is of the essence, or when you need quick, decisive action, and people are aware of and support the approach. It is best used when the outcome is extremely important and the relationship is of relatively low importance.
5. *Collaborate (I Win, You Win)*—This is where you cooperate with the other party to try to resolve a common problem to a mutually satisfying outcome. This is how you break free of the "win-lose" paradigm and seek the "win-win." This can be effective for complex scenarios where you need to find a novel solution. This can also mean re-framing the challenge to create a bigger space and room for everybody's ideas.

It is also central to try to match conflict strategies to differing situations. There are several variables that help define which strategy to employ to be most effective. Time sensitivity is an important variable. If there were never any time pressures, collaboration might always be the best approach to use. Issue priority is another variable as well as relational importance.

The Cost of Organizational Conflict

While every organization knows that workplace conflicts affect productivity and morale, the hard money drain of office drama is not as obvious. When CPP Inc. (2008), publishers of the Myers-Briggs Assessment and the Thomas-Kilmann Instrument, commissioned a study on workplace conflict, they found that U.S. employees spent 2.8 hours per week dealing with conflict. This amounts to approximately $359 billion in paid hours (based on average hourly earnings of $17.95) or the equivalent of 385 million working days. That's a lot of time spent gossiping, protecting turf, retaliating, recruiting people to one side or the other, planning defenses and navigating the drama. More importantly, that's time not spent answering customer questions, filling orders or doing the job employees were hired to do.

The ten largest costs of workplace conflict are as follows.

1. *Wasted time*—Research studies shows that up to 42 percent of employees' time is spent in engaging in or attempting to resolve conflicts.
2. *Bad decisions*—Making decisions requires that you have relevant information. Conflict contaminates the decision-making process.
3. *Lost employees*—Conflict accounts for up to 90 percent of the cause of involuntary terminations, except for staff reductions due to downsizing, mergers, and restructuring.
4. *Unnecessary restructuring*—Managers sometimes restructure the design and flow of tasks to reduce interaction between conflicting employees.
5. *Sabotage, theft, damage*—There is a direct correlation between the prevalence of workplace conflict and the amount of damage and theft to inventory and equipment.
6. *Lowered job motivation*—Motivation can be eroded by unrelieved stress of trying to get along with a "difficult" person.
7. *Lost work time*—Chronic conflict at the workplace is associated with absenteeism.
8. *Health costs*—Conflict-related job stress can cause illnesses and injuries that require medical attention under an employer's insurance plan.
9. *Toxic workplace*—Conflict can cause anger, fear, negativity, misunderstanding and distrust, and it may lower morale and strain work relationships.
10. *Grievances and lawsuits*—When conflict spirals out of control it can require third-party intervention, requiring more time, effort, and money.

The largest cost organizations may face in conflict situations is the expense of litigation and related claims. Well-managed conflict, on the other hand, leads to results that justify the importance and need for effective conflict management systems and processes.

Hidden Costs

Organizations that approach conflict with a strategic plan and concrete corporate structures utilize these to create strategic initiatives, more effective systems of communication, and greater commitment to the organization. The unresolved or escalating conflicts may lead to the above-mentioned costs. There are also hidden costs that can be more significant to the bottom line and the overall vigor of the organization: (1) time and salary loss—many studies suggest that close to 30 percent of a manager's time is spent dealing with employee conflict and helping employees reach agreement; (2) skill shortfalls—building relational skills, such as those associated with effective negotiation, interpersonal communication, and collaborative problem-solving, increases employees' ability to deal with conflict before it becomes destructive; (3) lack of data—company newsletters and department and company meetings may not be used effectively, and conflict arises from lack of information; and (4) ineffective conflict management or ADR approaches—many organizational cultures have little or no conflict management approaches in place. Effective processes should emphasize collaboration and consensus-building early in a dispute.

To ascertain evidence of these hidden costs, several commonly tracked employee metrics can provide the HR and conflict managers with a wealth of data to analyze and determine the true costs of conflict. Absenteeism, turnover and grievance filing are some indicators of workplace conflict and quantifying the costs of each of these factors can be used by managers to prove the added value of human resources interventions and trainings.

Gearing Up for Training and Development

Training is not just important to a company, it is crucial. Employee training and development are part of good management practices and good risk management strategies. At the same time as the need for employee training and development is increasing, it can be noted that the time and money available in organizations for traditional forms of learning such as formal training courses have decreased. Managing training and preparing for company change must involve identifying what issues impact organizational effectiveness. Several of these problem areas involve low productivity and output, lack of distinct goals and confusion about work assignment, lack of initiative and innovation, unclear decision making, no collaboration with varied working approaches, and poor internal working relations between departments and divisions.

Preparing for employee training and development programs helps with employee retention. In the book *Employee Training and Development*, Noe (2002) states: "Studies of what factors influence employee retention suggest that working with good colleagues, challenging job assignments and opportunities for career growth and development are among the top reasons for staying with a company."

Employee training and development programs prepare staffs to successfully carry out the mission of the organization where the workforce is more productive and requires less supervision. A workforce that engages in continuous learning is better able to meet the challenges of changes in the organization. Company training is an investment in the workforce. The benefits of a satisfied, well-trained team go far beyond a company's bottom line. Well-trained employees are more confident, committed, motivated, and loyal. When organizations make an investment in employees, employees will be more invested in the company's long-term goals and profits.

Managers, supervisors and team leaders will also need to assess their readiness for training. These individuals will need to consider the comfort level of sharing power with the team members and delegating decision-making to team members. Additional considerations are an examination of the feelings and attitudes about collaborative environments. Some of the areas of assessment will include discussions of the shortcomings and the successes of the team as well as the uncovering of any sensitive issues that may exist in the team. Finally, the training concept will include an assessment of the amount of buy-in and support that should be expected.

Two positive outcomes of training and development are improved worker satisfaction and morale and strengthening worker weaknesses. The investment in training that a company makes shows employees that they are valued and creates a supportive workplace. Most employees will have some weaknesses in their workplace skills. Training programs allow for the strengthening of those skills. The training goal is to bring all employees to a higher level, so they all have similar skills and knowledge. This necessary training can create an overall knowledgeable staff with employees who can work on teams or work independently without constant help and supervision from others.

Preparing and designing a training plan does not mean building a perfect plan. The major emphasis is to get started and the training plan can and will be adapted to the team, division or company's needs. Learning is always an ongoing process.

Leading Change

Harry Truman once said, "A leader has the ability to get other people to do what they don't want to do and like it." We must work hard to change an organization successfully to deal with internal and external conflicts. When we plan carefully and build the proper foundation, dealing with conflict can be much easier, and we can improve the chances of success. At Harvard University, Professor John Kotter (1996) established a change model that visualized how organizations could manage and implement change powerfully and successfully.

- *Create a sense of urgency*—For change to happen, it helps if the whole company really wants it. Develop a sense of urgency around the need for change.
- *Form a powerful and guiding coalition*—Convince people that change is necessary. This often takes strong leadership and visible support from key people within the organization.
- *Create a vision for change*—A clear vision can help everyone understand why you're asking them to do something about the issues of conflict.
- *Communicate the change vision*—Don't simply call special meetings to communicate the vision for conflict resolution. Instead, talk about it every chance you get. Use the vision daily to make decisions and solve problems.
- *Remove obstacles*—Put in place the structure for change and conflict resolution and continually check for barriers to it. Removing obstacles can empower the people you need to execute the vision, and it can help the change move forward.
- *Create short-term wins*—Nothing motivates more than success. When the organization gets a taste of victory early in the change process, larger win-win resolutions can follow.
- *Build on the change*—After every resolution, analyze what went right and what needs improving.

- *Anchor the changes in corporate culture*—The corporate culture determines what gets done, so the values that lead to conflict resolution must become part of the overall organizational structure.

There are many individual anecdotes of how ordinary people get extraordinary things done. Exemplary leadership can instill and bring organizational change (Kouzes and Posner, 2012). These types of leaders can challenge the process and seek out opportunities to change, grow, innovate and improve. They can often inspire a shared vision by appealing to values, interests, hopes, and dreams. Additionally, they will enable others to act to promote cooperative goals and build trust while modeling the way with examples that are consistent with shared values. Finally, exemplary leaders encourage the heart by recognizing and celebrating individual and team contributions and accomplishments regularly.

Leading change in an organization is meant to pursue excellence. Excellent and successful companies are smart on the basics. They allow innovation to take place at all levels in a complex structure. Innovative companies emerge through several attributes (Peters and Waterman, 1982).

They see a problem, come up with solutions and implement them. They attempt to stay close to the customer and learn from the people they serve. Autonomy and entrepreneurship exist to support many leaders and managers in the organization. Productivity is achieved through people who are seen as the root source of quality and gain. A basic tenet of these companies is that they are hands-on and value-driven, where workers walk the talk and support the company policies. They stick to the knitting and remain reasonably close to the business they know.

Interventions in organizations to create change can have some interesting results. Variables to be examined (Robertson, Roberts, and Porras, 1993) include (1) planned organizational change interventions that will generate positive changes in work setting variables; (2) the relationship between the amount of positive change in work setting variables and the amount of positive change in individual behavior will be positive; and (3) the relationship between the amount of positive change in individual behavior and the amount of positive change in the organizational outcomes will be positive.

The change leaders, conflict resolvers, human resource administrators and team leaders all must recognize that conflict is a growth industry. Everyone wants to participate in decisions that affect them. Roger Fisher and William Ury (2011) state that "the advent of the negotiation revolution has brought more conflicts, not less. Hierarchies tend to bottle up conflict, which comes out into the open as hierarchies give way to networks." They continue to say that in the form of business competition, conflict helps create prosperity, and it lies at the heart of the democratic process, where the best decisions result not from a superficial consensus but from examining different points of view and seeking out creative solutions.

Redefining Leadership

During the decade of the 1990s, in the face of numerous high-profile leadership failures among the ranks of business and political leaders, a popular philosophy began to emerge. As many of these leaders were discovered to be leading personal lives characterized by questionable behavior, the public was told that a leader's personal life does not necessarily have an impact on his or her exercise of leadership. The most important issue when selecting a leader is whether they can do the job (Rima, 2000). Do our leaders possess the experience and the ability to fill the position?

There is little doubt that the position and title of leader offers individuals authority and the power to make rules. However, leadership may have little to do with position or title; leadership is about solving problems and unlocking the potential in others. Excellent leaders are skilled collaborators. One cannot lead unless one understands how to work with people. There are many levels and degrees of leadership. Some basic models and principles of leadership (Gitomer, 2011) are to get the people who work for you to like and believe in you while ensuring that the employees and their jobs are a "fit." Good leadership involves allowing people to tell you their goals, then modifying them together. By giving people specific tasks and clear directions leaders engender a positive work attitude and pave the way for encouragement, reward and praise that could mitigate conflict or dispute instances.

Leadership is both similar and dissimilar to management. Leadership entails working with people to effect goal attainment. Management is concerned with order and stability to the organization. Organizational leaders in the company need to set direction and strategies; they must communicate goals and build working teams and divisions; they should energize and inspire subordinates while delegating authority to empower workers.

Redefined leadership is purposeful about how to confront and overcome biases and conflicts so that the organization can foster a culture of collaboration, discover common ground, and reach across our differences. The business world we live in has changed dramatically in the last decade. Companies are now witnessing a revolution in the way information is obtained and transmitted. This innovative information paradigm is changing the ways we relate to one another. The rapid rise of global, networked communities will redefine how we work, how we interact and how we lead others in the organization. Leaders will need to find new and creative ways to bring members of the workforce together to propel success. Leadership in this new era is not guaranteed; it must be earned. Technology is miraculous because it allows us to do more with less, ratcheting up our fundamental capabilities to a higher level (Thiel and Masters, 2015).

Resistance to Change

Managing change and stress is discussed later; however, with the rate of technological growth and the global economy, change is now the normal state of business. Although change management decisions are normally made at an executive level, it's still very important to have the rest of the employees bought into the change. Having employees who are opposed to what is going to be changing from the start is a major setback and one that needs to be dealt with carefully to be successful with the change management.

Many organizational change efforts fail to reach their objectives. The major reasons people resist change are they fear a loss of status or job security. They see a poorly aligned reward system that is paired with the fear of the unknown which can breed a climate of mistrust among the stakeholders. Workers, work teams, departments and project managers believe that the changes rely on faulty implementation methodology.

Employees resist change when it is introduced poorly to them, when it affects how they do their work, and when they don't see and understand the need for the changes. They also experience resistance to change when they are not involved in the decision to change or, at least, in making up the specific steps in the changes as they will affect them.

Organizations of all types constantly experience change, because as industries grow, businesses must evolve. Change needs to be dealt with in an effective and responsible manner, and if done correctly, it will seriously benefit the company and make it a smooth transition. Pragmatic change agents in organizations need to understand the reasons organizations resist change.

Every organization has its own culture. Some are casual, with a focus on the development of individual expression. Other firms stress regimented work processes. When change is introduced into either of these models, it can disrupt the cultural equilibrium.

There are many different organizational structures. Change will have to acknowledge and accommodate the company's set structure. Many organizations resist change because they don't want to lose their invested costs. Organizations fear the costs of change, which is why some are averse to moving quickly.

The resistance to change in some companies rubs against the organization's culture. Culture is not climate. The climate of resistance targets what the company's core values, beliefs, norms and behaviors are. The unwillingness to accept change may include the notions (Schwartz and Davis, 1981) that every organization has a culture, with separate cultures in different subgroups. The company culture reflects what has worked in the past. Another impression is that company strategies can be hidden, but culture can give insight to it. Well-run organizations have distinctive cultures that allow them to create, implement and maintain their leadership positions.

When the workforce resists change, is it because the employees feel that they are being shaped and molded by the change or do they feel they have a role in shaping the change? We have seen that the concept of change is extraordinarily complex. Organizational change is centered on the following propositions: (1) change requires both strong leadership and strong management; (2) no single type of leadership is best for creating, inducing, motivating and accomplishing change; and (3) each phase of the change process requires committed leaders.

Employee Resistance Is Challenging

Managing resistance to change is challenging for many reasons. Resistance to change can be covert or overt, organized or individual. Employees can realize that they don't like or want a change and resist publicly, verbally, and argumentatively. The adoption of changes in new ideas and techniques does not occur naturally but results from hard work and trial and error. It is important to recognize this fact and to try to develop information that is concise and reaches people who can use it.

Many avenues of communication should be used to promote the adoption of any change. Managers, supervisors and team leaders should not expect one report, one presentation, or one conference to accomplish everything. Some employees can forcefully resist to adopt the changes and bring the organization the need for confrontation and conflict resolution. Other employees can also feel uncomfortable with the changes introduced and resist, sometimes unknowingly, through the actions they take and the words they use to describe the change. Resistance affects the speed at which an organization adopts an innovation.

In short, workforce resistance affects productivity, quality, interpersonal communication, employee commitment to contribution, and relationships in the workplace. Zander (1950) offered four primary reasons for resistance to surface. The first theory states that if the nature of the change is unclear to the people who are going to be influenced by the change, there will be resistance. Second, if the change is open to a wide variety of interpretations, there will be resistance. Third, if those influenced feel strong forces are deterring them from changing, there will be resistance. Fourth, if the people influenced by the change have pressure to make it instead of having a say in the nature or the direction of the change, there will be resistance.

Clearly, when the workforce believes that their input is considered, they are less likely to experience resistance to change. Smart employers recognize that this is a given on the front end of any changes that employees are asked to make.

The best way to motivate people to help you fulfill your goals is to help them fulfill their goals—**Deepak Chopra**

3

Transformational Organizations

Why Organizations Fail

In her book *Leadership from the New Sciences*, author Margaret Wheatley (2006) states that "the power of an organization is the capacity generated by relationships and its real energy can only come into existence through relationships." She adds that power is energy and it needs to flow through the organization without being confined to functions or levels of hierarchy. Those who relate through coercion or in disregard of others create negative energy—conflict. Ten reasons why organizations and leaders fail are

- lack of shared vision, focus and purpose;
- lack of enterprise-wide communication;
- lack of organizational ambition and a strategic approach for getting there;
- lack of respect for others within the organization;
- failure to tap resources and inner talent, creativity and responsibility;
- failure to break down walls between divisions;
- lack of hope and spirit;
- failure to negotiate win-win resolutions;
- failure to resolve conflicts creatively; and
- failure to focus outside and see the customer/consumer.

Organizational conflicts have negative aspects attached to them. At their worst, they can create a solidly dysfunctional organization that exhibits the five dimensions mentioned by author Patrick Lencioni (2002).

Dysfunction #1: Absence of trust

The fear of being vulnerable with team members prevents the building of trust within the team. This outcome occurs when team members are reluctant to open up to one another and are unwilling to admit their mistakes, weaknesses, or need for help. Without a certain comfort level among team members, a foundation of trust is not possible. Trust lies at the heart of a functioning, cohesive team and can only happen when team members are willing to be completely vulnerable with one another. This includes saying things like "I'm sorry" or "Your idea was better than mine."

Dysfunction #2: Fear of conflict

Conflict is naturally uncomfortable, but productive conflict focused on concepts and ideas is essential for any great team and organization to grow. When teams have a foundation of vulnerability-based trust, conflict simply becomes an attempt to find the best possible solution in the shortest period. The desire to preserve artificial harmony stifles the occurrence of productive ideological conflict. Teams that are lacking trust are incapable of engaging in unfiltered debate about key issues. It creates situations where team conflict can easily turn into veiled discussions and back channel comments. In a work setting where team members do not openly air their opinions, conflict develops and inferior decisions result.

Dysfunction #3: Lack of commitment

Commitment is clarity around decisions, not consensus. With commitment, teams move forward with complete buy-in from every team member—including those who may initially disagree. The lack of clarity prevents team members from making decisions they will stick to. Without conflict, it is difficult for team members to commit to decisions, fostering an environment where ambiguity prevails. Lack of direction and commitment can make employees disgruntled and disenfranchised.

Dysfunction #4: Avoidance of accountability

The need to avoid interpersonal discomfort prevents team members from holding one another accountable. When they don't commit to a clear plan of action, even the most focused and driven individuals are hesitant to call their peers on actions and behaviors that may seem counterproductive to the overall good of the team. It's easy to avoid difficult conversations but calling out peers on performance or behaviors that might hurt the team is essential to productivity.

Dysfunction #5: Inattention to results

The pursuit of individual goals and personal status erodes the focus on collective success. One of the greatest challenges to team success is the inattention to results. Great teams ensure all members, regardless of their individual responsibilities and areas of expertise, are doing their best to help accomplish team goals. Team members naturally tend to put their own needs (e.g., ego, career development, recognition) ahead of the collective goals of the team when individuals are not held accountable. If a team has lost sight of the need for achievement, conflict brews and the organization will ultimately suffer.

When teams are working in harmony, these dysfunctions cease to cause problems. Lencioni's (2002) model highlights the results when the team lacks trust, and this should be the area that demands the most concentration.

To impede the pitfalls and trappings of dysfunction, organizations must develop and engage in the process of strategic planning. To address competitive challenges the strategic plan must focus on integrating its vision, goals, policies and actions into a cohesive entity. This strategic management planning must include the interpretation of information from internal sources, including financial business development, marketing, sales and operations; information from external sources such as industry practices and developments, technological developments and legal regulations and restrictions; and the development of strategies to deal with change and conflict as they relate to the overall functioning, expectations, and needs of the whole organization, its employees and other stakeholders.

After an organization has chosen a management strategy, it has to execute that strategy—make it come to life in its day-to-day workings (Noe et al., 2010). The basic premise behind strategy implementation is that "an organization has a variety of structural forms and organizational processes to choose from when implementing a given strategy." When seeking a competitive advantage, employees and managers must be able to maintain behavior that is free of conflict and distrust. Performance management that includes methods for identifying, reducing and resolving conflict will ensure that everyone is working to their potential and that the strategic, administrative and development goals of the organization are reached.

Failing organizations may be losers because their corporate vision is unclear and uninspiring. Losing organizations do not clearly articulate where they are headed and what they are trying to accomplish, despite what their online mission and vision statements say. Organizations may be doomed to failure and be filled with myriad conflicts if their bureaucratic structure is too multi-leveled with hard boundaries between these levels. Finally, companies that do not look forward and adopt ideation techniques and have no concern for knowledge management strategies will ultimately fail.

Transformational Leadership and Organizations

A current and popular approach in defining successful organizations has been the focus of much research since the early 1980s and was originally pioneered by Alan Bryman (1992). Transformational leadership is a process that changes and transforms people and is concerned with emotions, values, ethics, standards and long-term goals. Organizations that utilize this approach attempt to assess workers' motives and needs and strive to treat them as full human beings. These types of organizations move workers to accomplish more than what is usually expected of them. It is a systematic process that often incorporates highly charismatic leadership. Generally, transformational organizations and leaders focus on an optimistic future with an enthusiastic approach to see what is needed to be accomplished. Positive outlooks are stated that attest to the confidence that future aims will be met and no challenge is too difficult to accept (Senge, 2006).

Transformational leadership characteristics impact organizational growth in positive ways when the leaders can find motivation from within. These individuals possess the ability to enact difficult decisions that are aligned with the company values and objectives. Powerful leaders do not let their egos get in the way, especially when they undertake calculated risks while trusting their instincts.

Eight of the most transformational organizational leaders are

- William Randolph Hearst (Hearst Communications);
- Bill Gates (Microsoft);
- Jack Dorsey (Twitter);
- Peter Lynch (Fidelity);
- Howard Schultz (Starbucks);
- Doug McMillon (Walmart);
- Susan Alexander (Biogen); and
- Sundar Pichai (Google).

These transformational leaders and their organizations set out to empower their workers, managers and supervisors as they attempt to nurture change and raise their awareness of conflict issues and methods of resolving them. These types of organizations motivate their workforce to move to high standards, to transcend their own self-interests for the good of their team, department or division. There can be little negative criticism of companies that instill conflict resolution strategies as part of transformational leadership. However, if criticism need be levied, it is possible that these organizations can be abused by internal measures. Because this type of company is largely concerned with affecting and changing people's values and moving them to a different vision, it can be determined that some people may take exception to the new directions and initiatives. Challenges may be presented about the dynamics of change and if these changes are rooted in good change for all stakeholders and, eventually, for the company in general (Conger, 1999).

In early December 2018, *Billboard* magazine, an American entertainment media brand owned by the Billboard-Hollywood Reporter Media Group, a division of Eldridge Industries, announced a change in the editorial director leadership after a two-and-a-half-year vacancy. Ms. Hannah Karp stated that one of the first things she would tackle in this new position was to meet with all the teams to focus on international coverage and technology. As a transformational leader she indicated that she recognized the challenges of the competition—Spotify, Shazam and YouTube.

Transformational leadership can be seen when leaders and followers make each other advance to a higher level of morale and motivation and, through the strength of their vision and personality, transformational leaders are able to inspire followers to change expectations, perceptions, and motivations to work toward common goals.

Later, researcher Bernard M. Bass (1985) developed what is today referred to as Bass's Transformational Leadership Theory. According to Bass, transformational leadership can be defined based on the impact that it has on followers. Transformational leaders, Bass suggested, garner trust, respect, and admiration from their followers. He also suggested that there were four different components of transformational leadership: intellectual stimulation, individualized consideration, inspirational motivation and idealized influence.

Intellectual Stimulation—Transformational leaders not only challenge the status quo, they also encourage creativity among followers. The leader encourages followers to explore new ways of doing things and new opportunities to learn.

Individualized Consideration—Transformational leadership also involves offering support and encouragement to individual followers. In order to foster supportive relationships, transformational leaders keep lines of communication open so that followers feel free to share ideas and so that leaders can offer direct recognition of the unique contributions of each follower.

Inspirational Motivation—Transformational leaders have a clear vision that they can articulate to followers. These leaders are also able to help followers experience the same passion and motivation to fulfill these goals.

Idealized Influence—The transformational leader serves as a role model for followers. Because followers trust and respect the leader, they emulate this individual and internalize his or her ideals.

Leadership and Manager Differences

Attempting to define leadership accurately is not easy. We have all experienced leadership that was good as well as bad, but we understand that with leadership comes power. Generally, power can be defined as the capacity to produce effects on others or the potential to influence others. Power is the product of interpersonal relationships, not of the individuals involved in them. Leadership is the exercise of that capacity.

Leadership is not the same as authority and is different from management. Abraham Zaleznik (1977) specified the major differences between leaders and managers. The difference between managers and leaders, he wrote, lies in the conceptions they hold, deep in their psyches, of chaos and order. Managers embrace process, seek stability and control, and instinctively try to resolve problems quickly, sometimes before they fully understand a problem's significance. Leaders, in contrast, tolerate chaos and lack of structure and are willing to delay closure to understand the issues more fully. As a Harvard Business School professor emeritus, Dr. Zaleznik was skilled in the practice of psychoanalysis and an admirer of the insights of Sigmund Freud. Below is a comparison table examining leaders and managers.

Dimension for Comparison	Leaders	Managers
Attitude toward goals	Personal and active	Impersonal, reactive, passive
Conceptions of work	Projecting ideas into images that excite people; developing options	An enabling process of coordinating and balancing; limiting options
Relations with others	Prefer solitary activities; relate intuitively and empathetically	Prefer to work with people; relate to them accordingly
Senses of self	Feel separate from their environment; depend on personal mastery of events for identity	Belong to their environment; depend on memberships, roles, and so on for identity

Exemplary Leadership

Many of us find ourselves on predictable paths of how things have been, how things are, and how they will be. The status quo is forged by the synaptic associations in our brains, beliefs, and assumptions. Exemplary leaders are not content with the predictable path; they dare to look beyond the status quo to imagine different outcomes than the one the predictable path leads to; they blaze new paths (Bielenberg, Burn, Galle, & Dickinson, 2016).

An observable set of leadership skills and abilities can indicate exemplary leadership in organizations that addresses best practices enabling companies to grow, progress and move forward unhindered by conflict. Exemplary leaders continually search for opportunities to change the status quo. They search for innovative ways to improve the organization. In doing so, they experiment and take risks. Leaders know that risk taking involves mistakes and failures, and they can accept the inevitable disappointments as learning opportunities.

Leaders establish principles concerning the way all stakeholders should be treated and the way goals should be pursued. Standards of excellence are created and set as examples for others to follow. To establish these standards and model the way effectively, operational plans must be in place. Excellent leaders steer projects along a predetermined course, measure performance, give feedback, meet budgets and schedules, and take corrective action (Kouzes and Posner, 1995). Because the prospect of complex change can overwhelm people and stifle action, leaders set interim goals so that people can achieve small wins as they work toward larger objectives. They unravel bureaucracy when it impedes action; they put up signposts when people are unsure of where to go or how to get there; and they create opportunities for victory.

Exemplary leadership behaviors will always make a profound positive difference in people's commitment and motivation, their work performance, and the success of their company. Two major behaviors exhibited by great leaders are (1) fostering collaboration by building trusting relationships, knowing that without trust, you can't lead, and that trust is the key to productive relationships, and relationships with peers, constituents and customers are key to great businesses; and (2) strengthening others by developing their competence. Exemplary leaders spend more time supporting and mentoring their constituents to develop their competence and confidence and then delegate effectively with accountability.

Clearly, some individuals are better than others as leaders. In many organizations there are tendencies to assign credit or blame for successes and failures to company leaders. These favorable or unfavorable outcomes have been labeled by J. Richard Hackman (2002) as "leader attribution error." Many times, the good or bad outcomes have nothing to do with the leader but are a result of the team members themselves for they are the ones who worked together to generate the product or service. However, in some cases a team leader's actions do really spell the difference between success and failure. Effective leaders (Hackman, 2002) make certain they have established work teams that will have stability over time while providing these teams with compelling direction. These leaders fine-tune the structure of teams to foster, rather than impede, teamwork. They also strive to tweak organizational structures, so they provide teams with ample support and resources. Many will arrange for and provide expert coaching to help teams.

Involving workforce members as participants in the leadership process moves these employees into a consultative role within a project, department, division or task-oriented team. By encouraging and supporting employees in their efforts to share the leadership function, exemplary leaders delegate tasks and they can be unencumbered and can focus on other issues.

Differences Among Workers, Managers and Leaders

Extensive sets of personal work habits and behaviors can often impede and block successful projects from reaching fruition. Basic content skills in communications, problem-solving and conflict resolution skills can drive employees, managers and leaders to adequately achieve organizational goals. Bruce Peltier (2010) succinctly outlines the key differences among workers, managers and leaders.

Worker	Manager	Leader
Performs basic tasks	Controls things	Creates things
Needs and uses resources	Budgets, makes ends meet	Finds resources
Interacts with peers	Interacts internally, keeps people in line with systems	Interacts with outsiders, inspires people
Responsible for own effort	Responsible for performance of organization	Responsible for overall outcome
Lacks overarching viewpoint	Creates structure, is risk averse	Create mandates, is a risk taker
Takes direction from others	Uses authority and rules	Uses influence, convinces
Provides feedback to organization	Monitors organizational culture	Monitors outside culture

Organizational Measurement

Business executives understand that their organization's measurement system strongly affects the behavior of managers and employees. During a year-long research project, Kaplan and Norton (1992) surveyed 12 companies to give managers complex information at a glance. They put the findings into a "balanced scorecard."

How do customers see us?	The customer perspective.
What must we excel at?	The internal perspective.
Can we continue to improve and create value?	Innovation and learning perspective.
How do we look to shareholders?	Financial perspective.

Measuring performance is a vital part of monitoring an organization's progress. The actual performance outcomes of an organization are measured against its intended goals. The strategic plan provides performance targets for the organization and sets the corporate direction.

Transformational leaders are capable of aligning business activities with deep vision and strategy and desire to improve internal and external communication while monitoring performance against organizational goals. The "balanced scorecard" assists with the examination of (1) profitability, (2) meeting customer expectations, (3) improvement of products and policies, (4) workforce training and corporate culture, and (5) translating the mission statement into specific measures.

Strategy mapping describes how an organization intends to create value for its shareholders. If the company's intangible assets represent more than 75 percent of its value, then strategy formulation and execution need to explicitly address the mobilization and alignment of intangible assets (Kaplan and Norton, 2004). Strategy maps are communication tools created by organization leaders and teams that are used to explain how value is created. They show a logical, step-by-step connection between strategies and objectives in the form of a cause-effect chain. The basic principles Kaplan and Norton described are that strategy balances contradictory forces and eventually reduces conflict. Strategy is based on a differentiated customer value proposition with a clear articulation of the strategy. Value is created through internal business processes that include an analysis of customer acquisition, satisfaction, retention, loyalty, and growth. Strategy consists of simultaneous, complementary themes that present a view of the operational process, innovative process, and regulatory and social process. Strategic alignment determines the value of intangible assets such as an examination of learning and growth, workforce skills and talents, teamwork and knowledge management.

Workplace Communication

> *Our lives begin to end the day we become silent about things that matter*—Dr. Martin Luther King, Jr.

Communication is the sharing and conveyance of information between two or more individuals. Effective communication requires all components interworking perfectly for delivering shared meaning. The workplace is a context in which all forms of communication take place and all types of relationships are seen. Organizational communication is the process through which members develop, maintain, and modify practices through their communication with all stakeholders. It can be considered as task-oriented and goal-oriented and is the basis for the development of relationships at work (Keyton, 2011).

When you are part of an organization, you endeavor to learn the rules and norms of that company. My colleague Joe DeVito (2019) has broken down workplace communication into four major types. First, lateral communication refers to message between equals—for example, worker to worker, project leader to project leader. These messages may move within the same department of the organization or across divisions. Second, upward communication consists of messages sent from lower levels of an organizational hierarchy to upper levels—for example, field workers to program managers or from faculty member to dean. This type of communication is often concerned with work-related activities and problems, ideas for change and suggestions for innovative improvements. Third, downward communication consists of messages sent from the highest levels to the lowest levels of the hierarchy. Common forms of downward communication include explanations of procedures, goals and changes, and company orders.

Grapevine messages, the fourth type of workplace communication, do not follow any of the formal lines of communication established in an organization. Much like grapevines, they seem to have a life of their own and wander into all different directions. These types of messages address topics that you want to discuss in a more interpersonal setting, such as issues that have not yet been made public or finalized.

As a communications professor for over thirty years, teaching speech and interpersonal communication, I have often grappled with three complex questions: (1) Are there any systematic patterns of human communication that lead to development of solid relations? (2) Are there strategies and initiatives that assist in the building and destruction of these relationships? (3) What can we learn about the answers to the first two questions that will help us to manage our interactions at work, deal with successes and failures, and address common conflict areas?

Clinical professor of finance and psychologist Bruce Tuckman (1965) first came up with the memorable phrase "forming, storming, norming, and performing" in his article "Developmental Sequence in Small Groups." He used it to describe the path that most teams follow on their way to high performance. Later, he added a fifth stage, "adjourning" (which is sometimes known as "termination").

Forming: The work team meets and learns about the opportunities and challenges, and then agrees on goals and begins to work on tasks. Members may behave quite independently and be motivated. Members attempt to become oriented to the tasks as well as to one another. Discussion centers on defining the scope of the task and how to approach it. To grow from this stage to the next, each member must relinquish the comfort of non-threatening topics and risk the possibility of conflict.

Storming: In this stage of work team development, the members of the group start to gain each other's trust. This stage often starts when they voice their opinions. Positive and polite atmospheres contribute to different feelings of excitement, eagerness and positiveness, while others may have feelings of suspicion and anxiety. Disagreements and personality clashes must be resolved before the team can progress out of this stage, and so some teams may never emerge from storming or re-enter that phase if new challenges or disputes arise. This phase can become destructive to the team and will lower motivation if allowed to get out of control. Questions may arise about who is going to be responsible for what, what the rules are, what the reward system is, and what criteria for evaluation are. These reflect conflicts over leadership, structure, power, and authority.

Norming: Gradually, the team moves into the norming stage. This is when people start to resolve their differences, appreciate colleagues' strengths, and respect the authority of the team leader. People develop a stronger commitment to the team goal, and progress can develop and grow. There is often a prolonged overlap between storming and norming, because, as new tasks come up, the team may lapse back into behavior from the storming stage. Creativity is high at this stage; data flow and cohesion are attained by the group members and their interactions are characterized by openness and sharing of information on both a personal and task level. They feel good about being part of an effective group.

Performing: The team reaches the performing stage when hard work leads to the achievement of the team's goal. The structures and processes that have been set up support this well. Organizational leaders can delegate much of the work, and then they can concentrate on developing team members. There is unity and group identity and the overall goal is productivity through problem-solving and work.

Adjourning: Many teams will reach this stage eventually. For example, project teams exist for only a fixed period, and even permanent teams may be disbanded through organizational restructuring. Concluding a group can create some apprehension. The most effective interventions in this stage are those that facilitate task termination and the disengagement process. This final stage was added in 1975 by Bruce Tuckman 10 years after the initial four stages. The end of the group, also referred to as the "mourning" or "adjourning" stage, is seen to be a bittersweet accomplishment by many of the group's members. They may share their experience of the process with one another and share with each other the insight and hope they have acquired throughout the experience. Positive accomplishments are celebrated.

In "How I Learned to Let My Workers Lead," Ralph Stayer (1990) describes how he learned to let his workers lead at this family business, Johnsonville Sausage. Stayer observed that despite his company's financial success, the employees were bored with their roles and took no responsibility for their work. They appeared in the morning, did their work and went home. Stayer realized that he had been focused entirely on the financial side of the business and return on assets and had seen people only as dutiful tools. The business had grown adequately, and that very success was the biggest obstacle to change.

He had made all the decisions about purchasing, scheduling, quality, pricing, marketing, sales, hiring, and all the rest of it. Now the very things that had brought success, the centralized control, belligerent behavior, and authoritarian business practices, were creating the environment that made the CEO so unhappy.

Stayer had been Johnsonville Sausage, assisted by some hired hands who lacked commitment. They had no stake in the company and no power to make decisions or control their own work. The norming, forming and performing stages were suffering. To improve results, he had to increase their involvement in the business. The transformation of Johnsonville Sausage from a profitable, traditionally-managed company to an innovative and growing organization came about from the relinquishing of control and empowering the workforce to be all they wanted to be. Stayer observed that performance grew because

- ✓ people want to be great;
- ✓ performance hinges on individuals' expectations;
- ✓ expectations are driven by things like vision, goals, compensations and decision making, and the actions of managers shape expectations;
- ✓ learning is an ongoing process; and
- ✓ performance changes are made when the workforce change themselves first [reprinted by permission of Harvard Business School Publishing, 12/2018].

Success with workplace communication results in productivity and satisfaction in both personal and business relationships, and that success comes from our ability to both collaborate with one another and resolve conflicts when they arise.

Workplace Channels and Networks

Much like the television broadcasting industry, a single TV channel services a local area and provides its viewers with news and programming of interest to that community. By contrast, a TV network is a large distribution center that delivers content to member channels (often called affiliates). At an organization a communication channel refers specifically to the means by which messages are transmitted between and among coworkers. These small channel communications can take the form of face-to-face communication, written communication such as memos and e-mails, and telephone calls and instant messaging.

Communication networks usually consist of the formal patterns of interactions that regulate how the company stakeholders talk to each other (i.e. company newsletters, web-postings, video-conferencing). When these networks are used effectively, they serve as a source of work support in helping people develop skills and acquire knowledge (Allen & Finkelstein, 2003). When used ineffectively, these communication networks can cause conflict, stress, lowered workplace morale, and less productivity. To become a functional member of any workplace, individuals must develop an understanding of the communication practices that it comprises.

Many of these practices include how the organization culture is defined, how workers are oriented and socialized into the organization, how coworkers develop relationships with each other, and how individuals express and resolve disagreements.

Organizational assimilation involves the processes by which individuals become integrated into an organization. Given that most individuals join numerous organizations throughout the course of their lifetime, organizational assimilation is a ubiquitous aspect of workers' lives. However, assimilating or integrating into an organization is neither simple nor guaranteed. Unsuccessful assimilation has been linked to premature turnover, costly to both organizations and newcomers. Therefore, facilitating and overseeing the assimilation of new workers is a significant function of management. This insight gives managers, members, and other stakeholders an ability to better anticipate and facilitate newcomers' successful assimilation. This can result in fewer conflict flare-ups. There are three phases in the assimilation process: anticipatory socialization, organizational encounter, and metamorphosis.

> **Anticipatory socialization**: In this stage newcomers form expectations of the organization and what it would be like to become a member of that organization. During this stage most new workers develop a set of expectations and beliefs about how people communicate formally and informally in a particular organization.
>
> **Organizational encounter**: This stage involves the member entering and becoming acquainted with the new organization and occurs when the employee confronts the reality of his or her organizational role. The new member, while already formally admitted within the organization, has not yet become socially accepted as a trustworthy or dependable member in the eyes of their coworkers. Organizational encounter mainly consists of the newly admitted employee seeking and receiving information in order to become more familiar with the processes regarding the organization.
>
> **Metamorphosis**: This stage involves the psychological adjustment that occurs when uncertainty has been managed and the workers' priorities move from being preoccupied with their transition to maintaining their new situations. The worker begins to alter his or her priorities so that they are in line with the values of the organization. He or she can negotiate some aspects of their role at the organization, but for the most part they must adapt to the standards already in place.

To assess one's assimilation into the workplace, the following questionnaire was designed by Bernadette M. Gailliard (2010) and Karen Meyers and David Seibold:

The Organizational Assimilation Index
Reprinted by permission of SAGE Publications 11/2010

The following 24 statements concern your assimilation into the workplace. Indicate the extent to which you agree with each statement according to the following scale:

If you **strongly agree** with the statement, write 5 in the blank.

If you **agree** with the statement, write 4 in the blank.

If you **neither agree nor disagree** with the statement, write 3 in the blank.

If you **disagree** with the statement, write 2 in the blank.

If you **strongly disagree** with the statement, write 1 in the blank.

__3__ 1. I feel like I know my supervisor pretty well.
__4__ 2. My supervisor sometimes discusses problems with me.
__2__ 3. My supervisor and I talk together often.
__4__ 4. I consider my coworkers friends.
__4__ 5. I feel comfortable talking to my coworkers.
__4__ 6. I feel like I know my coworkers pretty well.
__4__ 7. I understand the standards of my organization.
__4__ 8. I think I have a good idea about how my organization operates.
__4__ 9. I know the values of my organization.
__4__ 10. I do not mind being asked to perform my work according to the organization's standards.
__3__ 11. My supervisor recognizes when I do a good job.
__4__ 12. My supervisor listens to my ideas.
__4__ 13. I think my supervisor values my opinions.
__4__ 14. I think my supervisor recognizes my value to the organization.
__3__ 15. I talk to my coworkers about how much I like it here.
__4__ 16. I volunteer for duties that benefit the organization.
__3__ 17. I talk about how much I enjoy my work.
__4__ 18. I often show others how to perform my work.
__3__ 19. I think I am an expert at what I do.
__4__ 20. I have figured out efficient ways to do my work.
__4__ 21. I can do others' jobs, if I am needed.
__4__ 22. I have changed some aspect of my position.
__4__ 23. I do this job a bit differently than my predecessor did.
__3__ 24. I have helped to change the duties of my position.

Scoring:

Add your scores for items 1, 2, and 3. This is your *familiarity with supervisors* score. 9

Add your scores for items 4, 5, and 6. This is your *familiarity with coworkers* score. 12

16 Add your scores for items 7, 8, 9, and 10. This is your *acculturation* score.

15 Add your scores for items 11, 12, 13, and 14. This is your *recognition* score.

Add your scores for items 15, 16, and 17. This is your *involvement* score.
Add your scores for items 18, 19, 20, and 21. This is your *job competency* score.
Add your scores for items 22, 23, and 24. This is your *role negotiation* score.

Add your scores for all 24 items. This is your overall *organizational assimilation* score.

In summary, to be assimilated and socialized effectively into the workplace, individuals progress through various stages that allow workers to transform from an organizational outsider to be an effective member who can perform his or her organizational role.

Power and Influence

Power and influence are two very different terms with several differences in meaning. Power can be defined as the authority to get something done, the ability to influence or control events. This usually evokes fear. Power can be used to achieve a goal such as the completion of a task. However, since power is often associated with fear, there is a tendency for the task to be completed poorly, especially when the person who uses the power is absent. Many times, the quality of work decreases. Supervisors and managers need to accept and cultivate power and develop and perfect ways to use it judiciously and appropriately. They must realize that misapplication of either can result in the loss of both and can cause, provoke and stimulate tension and conflict. Power depends on the relationship and the success of using power will depend on the values that individuals have to offer. Power is contextual as in the fact that your potential to influence depends on the context of the relationship.

Morton Deutsch (1973) described power as a relational concept functioning between the person and his or her environment. Power, therefore, is determined not only by the characteristics of the person or persons involved in any given situation, nor solely by the characteristics of the situation, but by the interaction of these two sets of factors. He also stated that three types of power can be *environmental power*, the degree to which an individual can favorably influence his or her overall environment; *relationship power*, the degree to which a favorably influence another person; and *personal power*, the degree a person is able to satisfy his or her own desires.

The classic framework of sources of power comes from French and Raven (1959).

1. *Legitimate*—This comes from the belief that a person has the formal right to make demands and to expect others to be compliant and obedient. Legitimate power is related to the position or status of the person in the organization. Legitimate power gives the leader/manager power over their direct reports. The more senior a person is and/or the more people they may have in their team, the more positional power the person perceives that they have. All managers have some degree of positional power.
2. *Reward*—This is a result of one person's ability to compensate another for compliance. Examples of these rewards are promotions, pay increases, working on special projects, training and developmental opportunities and compliments. Reward power is the result of positional power and can be limited to one's position in the organization.
3. *Expert*—This is based on a person's high levels of skill and knowledge. Expert power refers to the power that people have who have specialist knowledge, who are experts in their field or who have knowledge or skills that are in short supply. People tend to listen more to those who demonstrate expertise. Expert power does not require positional power.
4. *Referent*—This is the result of a person's perceived attractiveness, worthiness and right to others' respect. Referent power is the ability of others to identify with those who have desirable resources or personal charismatic traits.
5. *Coercive*—This comes from the belief that a person can punish others for noncompliance. Coercive power is the opposite of reward power. It is the ability to use threats and punishments. Many managers and leaders abuse this source of power, which leads to greater problems. Coercion tends to damage working relationships.
6. *Informational*—This is a result of a person's ability to control the information that others need to accomplish something. This power may be insider power that becomes vitally important when shared.

Influence can be defined as the ability to have an impact on the beliefs and actions of an individual. It is the ability to affect ideas and actions. Influence evokes respect. Unlike power, influence contains a mystic charm that those under the influence keep working in the desired manner even in the absence of the influential person. This charm involves connecting—the ability to identify with people and relate to them in a way that increases one's influence with them.

Influence is a desirable trait in any leader. Both power and influence are attributes that we come across very early in our lives. Power and influence are separate entities, contrary to common perception. Though many times it looks like the person with authority is influential because of his or her power, often the opposite is true. There are differences between power and influence though their ultimate purpose or objective is the same, and that is to control others or to get them to do things you want them to do.

Influence and power are never the property of an individual; they belong to a group and remain in existence only so long as the group keeps together (Arendt, 1969). In some organizations there are subtle and not-so-subtle power/influence plays made by separate divisions. The sales division, claiming they drive the company's profit base, may feel they are more important than the public relations division. This relational view of power and influence causes discontent, jealousy and conflict within the employees in the divisions and the organization.

In a power process, *relational* power is the perception of one's ability to influence others in a specific relationship. Relational power stems from the relationship between and among coworkers. It is a judgment of the potential influence someone may have in relation to another person. Relational power is generally experienced one of three ways: an individual's capacity to shape the relational environment; an individual's ability to utilize the relationship to bring a vision to manifestation; and the individual's capacity to maintain the relationship over time. The power to control or influence others resides in the control over things that individuals value, which may range all the way from specific resources to personal support (Emerson, 1962).

Relative power, on the other hand, is not an examination of the power process but a comparison of two or more such processes or potential processes. It is a perceived capacity to bring one's vision to fruition in comparison to others at a specific point in a specific environment.

As an example, in the United States the issue of legalization of marijuana is presently being debated. Some states have legalized marijuana while others have not. The federal government has not legalized marijuana. Those states that have legalized marijuana have done so despite the federal government's policies. At present, the states are expressing high

To be successful, one needs to identify the sources of power in negotiations and use these sources effectively. Power and leverage in negotiating means the ability to exercise authority and influence. The ability or perceived ability to get things done is also power.

When seeking to gain leverage and conduct successful conflict discussions, it is most helpful to: (1) identify the facts of the other party; (2) discover what the other party wants by asking open-ended questions; (3) reduce a sense of urgency to settle; and (4) be open to saying "no" to the other side's demands.

Sharing Power in Organizations

To improve an organization's climate, change in the dimension of power needs to be forthcoming from those who wield the power. Good leaders build powerful teams by sharing power, not by building themselves up (falsely) by imagining they can hoard power personally.

Power is shared out of necessity more than out of concern for principles of organizational development or participatory democracy. Power is shared because no one person controls all the desired activities in an organization (Salancik and Pfeffer, 2011). Because power derives from activities rather than individuals, the power is never absolute and derives ultimately from the specific context of the situation. In one library I studied in Westchester County in New York, I saw this principle in action. This library was planning to upgrade the infrastructure—new tables, efficient windows, new book stacks, and electrical upgrades. The managers and executives surveyed the existing plans and the architectural blueprints. When the work was completed, the main opposition to the new changes came from the librarians, who were not consulted on the upgrade.

The managers who wielded the power over this project did not share power decisions and failed to incorporate electrical upgrades that supported all the new computer technology in the library. In the end, the librarians needed to string extension cords over existing lighting fixtures to accommodate the electrical needs of the technology. If organizational leaders take the higher road of sharing power and building powerful teams, they gain real power. They can end up with a cadre of people who provide and do great things to make the company succeed.

Here are four practical ways that sharing power plays out (Azzarello, 2012).

1. Human vs. boss

If the thinking starts with "We're both humans" vs. "I'm the boss and you are the worker," there is the creation of an environment where everyone feels acknowledged. If special privileges that only the boss gets are flaunted, everyone else feels resentful and will not bring their best to the business.

Spending personal time with people in the trenches, on the assembly line, on the help desk shows that you understand and value all the jobs in your organization and you are not "above it all." It builds tremendous loyalty because when you ask someone to do work for you, they know you appreciate what you are asking them to do. It is hard to overestimate the value of this as a leader.

2. Curious vs. right

People protecting their power need to be right and to stay right. So it's not just that they are not good listeners, they need to not listen. Leaders who are genuinely curious invite new ideas and are always learning. They learn what is really going on in their organization and therefore know what is causing inefficiency, frustration, and suffering—so they can fix it.

The "right" executive doesn't want to hear it. They are right often enough that they can succeed to a certain extent, but they miss the opportunity to recognize breakthroughs that others might contribute.

3. Promote others vs. inflate yourself

Leaders who take credit for their organizations' work are, again, trying to hold on to false personal power. Leaders who promote and elevate their stars build a much higher value organization. Solid leaders give workers recognition and help them move up and then the entire organization gets stronger.

4. Open vs. secret

People protecting personal power are secretive. They believe that if they know more than everyone else, they will remain more important. Real leaders communicate a lot. They make it a point to share as much information as possible with everybody. They see additional power in having a well-informed team that can contribute more because they know more.

Effective organizational leaders win people over by building an open environment of trust and respect. They create meaning for people so they can feel proud of their work. They offer personal recognition. They go out of their way to make the work matter to the people doing it.

Powerful people in organizations must value the input of others and focus on resolving problems. Those of us who have participated when powerful people have solicited our input may have experienced three outcomes (Cahn & Abigail, 2014): (1) our ideas are utilized, which makes us feel good; (2) our ideas are not used, but we are provided with an explanation as to why not, which makes us realize that the situation was more complicated than we realized; and (3) our ideas are not used because power sharing was a pretense on the part of the more powerful person.

Power and Politics

There are few business activities more prone to a credibility gap than the way in which executives approach organizational life. A sense of disbelief occurs when managers purport to make decisions in rationalistic terms while most observers and participants know that personalities and politics play a significant if not an overriding role. Whatever else organizations may be, they are political structures. This means that organizations operate by distributing authority and setting a stage for the exercise of power. It is no wonder, therefore, that individuals who are highly motivated to secure and use power find a familiar and hospitable environment in business (Zaleznick, 1970)

At the same time, executives are reluctant to acknowledge the place of power both in individual motivation and in organizational relationships. Somehow, power and politics are dirty words, and in linking these words to the play of personalities in organizations, some managers withdraw into the safety of organizational logics.

Organizations provide a power base for individuals. From a purely economic standpoint, organizations exist to create a surplus of income over costs by meeting needs in the marketplace. But organizations also are political structures which provide opportunities for people to develop careers and therefore provide platforms for the expression of individual interests and motives. The development of careers, particularly at high managerial and professional levels, depends on accumulation of power as the vehicle for transforming individual interests into activities which influence other people.

Besides the conditions of scarcity and competition, politics in organizations grows out of the existence of constituencies. A superior may be content himself with shifts in the allocation of resources and consequently power, but he represents subordinates who, for their own reasons, may be unhappy with the changes. These subordinates affirm and support their boss. They can also withdraw affirmation and support and consequently isolate the superior with all the painful consequences this entails.

Still another factor that heightens the competition for power that is characteristic of all political structures is the incessant need to use whatever power one possesses. Corporations have an implicit "banking" system in power transactions. The initial "capitalization" which makes up an individual's power base consists of three elements: (1) the quantity of formal authority vested in his or her position relative to other positions; (2) the authority vested in his or her expertise and reputation for competence (a factor weighted by how important the expertise is for the growth areas of the corporation against the historically stable areas of its business); and (3) the attractiveness of his or her personality to others (a combination of respect for him or her as well as liking him or her, although these two sources of attraction are often in conflict).

Successful organizations balance employee needs with their own demands for performance and that centers on cooperative endeavors and common purposes. The realities of experience in organizations, on the other hand, show that conflicts of interest exist among people who ultimately share a common fate and are supposed to work together. What makes business more political and less ideological and rationalistic is the overriding importance of conflicts of interest. Conflicts of interest in the competition for resources are easily recognized as, for example, in capital budgeting or in allocating money for research and development. But these conflicts can be subjected to bargaining procedures which all parties to the competition validate by their participation.

Organizational life within a political frame is a series of contradictions. It is an exercise in rationality, but its energy comes from the ideas in the minds of power figures, the contents of which, as well as their origins, are only dimly perceived. It deals with sources of authority and their distribution. Yet it depends in the first place on the existence of a balance of power in the hands of an individual who initiates actions and gets results.

It has many rituals associated with it, such as participation, democratization, and the sharing of power, yet the real outcome is the consolidation of power around a central figure to whom other individuals make emotional attachments.

Any collective experience, such as organizational life with its capacity for charging the atmosphere in the imagery of power conflicts, can fall victim to rigidities. These rigidities consist mainly of the formation and elaboration of structures, procedures, and other ceremonials which create the illusion of solving problems but only give people something to act on to discharge valuable energies.

Some employees believe that politics and power in the workplace are a game that corporate and management play. However, games usually have rules to follow, a referee or judge, and an ending with a winner. Although politics has a winner, this game never ends, the rules are always subject to change, and there is no referee or spokesperson.

One part of organizational politics includes the manipulation of an individual to get other employees to perform or act as the manipulator desires. The other part of the organizational politics game is the negotiation and cooperation with or resistance to the manipulator. Politics can assist or harm an employee, depending on his or her decision to play the game. Employees must understand that politics is a power scheme game that is combined with other power schemes. Some things are accomplished by following organizational procedures, while other things are accomplished politically.

Political behaviors are activities that are not required as part of an employee's formal role in the organization. These behaviors influence or attempt to influence the distribution of advantages or disadvantages within the organization. Politics are a fact of life in all organizations. Politics will always be a part of an organization, as long as people are involved. Organizational politics may decrease job satisfaction, increase turnover and reduce productivity in the workforce.

Stakeholders compete for the resources that an organization produces. Shareholders want dividends, employees want raises. An organization must manage both cooperation and competition among stakeholders to grow and survive. All stakeholders have a common goal of organizational survival, but not all goals are identical. Organizational conflict often occurs when a stakeholder group pursues its interests at the expense of other stakeholders. Given the different goals of stakeholders, organizational conflict is inevitable. Conflict is associated with negative images, such as unions getting angry and violent, but some conflict can improve effectiveness. When conflict passes a certain point, it hurts an organization (Jones, 2011).

How would you handle the following situation at work?

Working with Leslie

You walk into work one day, and the first person you see is Leslie moving into the workspace right next to yours. You walk quietly by, settle in at your workplace, and think to yourself, "How can this be happening?" You have tried everything you know to avoid Leslie—even transferring out of a department. It looks like Leslie has been transferred into your new department and you are going to have to work with this person every day. To make matters worse, you just looked at your e-mail, and your supervisor has informed you that Leslie is now your direct report and working for you and your team.

Questions:

Assuming that Leslie's style is the very opposite of yours, answer the following questions:

- What are you going to have to do so that you can work with Leslie?

_____
_____

- How would you work out some form of agreement with Leslie so that you don't have conflict?

_____
_____

- As Leslie's supervisor, what role(s) would power play in your communications, interactions, and decisions?

_____
_____

Managing Change and Stress

Change in organizations is the norm, while stability is not. Clearly change can cause stress, but stress should be a powerful driving force, not an obstacle. Any organization or, for that matter, relationship that is not changing continuously will disappear or suffer or it will have to undergo massive and painful reorganization to modernize its management practices. Ongoing change leads to innovation and adaptation and stronger human connections. Not changing produces failure and periodic trauma, including personal break-ups, outsourcing of jobs, closures and downsizing.

Organizational change management undergoes three phases. First is preparing for the change and it includes activities to contemplate the best strategies for the change. In this stage the stakeholders assess the scope of the change, the readiness of the organization, the required project resources, and the strengths of the team(s). The second phase is managing the change, which includes designing the organizational change management plans and individual change management activities. It includes executing the plans and implementing the change into the organization. The last phase is reinforcing the change. After implementing changes using change management activities, this phase assesses the results, celebrates successes, and conducts "after-action" interviews (Hiatt and Creasey, 2012).

Location, gender, environment, and many other factors contribute to the build-up of stress. Job stress results from the interaction of the worker and the conditions of his or her work. Differences in individual characteristics such as personality and coping skills can be very important in predicting whether certain job conditions will result in stress. In other words, what is stressful for one person may not be a problem for someone else. This viewpoint underlies prevention strategies that focus on workers and ways to help them cope with demanding job conditions. In general, occupational stress is caused by a mismatch between perceived effort and perceived reward and/or a sense of low control in a job with high demands. Psychosocial stressors are a major cause of occupational stress.

The stress we feel in our lives when confronted with change often erupts into conflict with our coworkers and managers. Stress is always an escalator in a conflict. In many cases the stress is the tension generated from a work event that appears unmanageable. Stress exacerbated by organizational change varies based on the individual and situation. Most stress is temporary, although there are situations where stress can last for a long time. For example, people who work in sales and advertising generally find that there are high levels of stress associated with their careers; in these cases, stress must be managed. Everyday life is full of environmental stressors that can cause minor irritations. Work-related stress occasionally arises when demands exceed abilities.

- *Stressors* are the sources of stress (Cahn & Abigail, 2014).
- *Eustress*, a good kind of stress, is a short-term stress that encourages us to expend more energy on important activities and take them more seriously.
- *Hypostress*, or underload, happens when we're bored or unchallenged by our situations. Eustress and hypostress are only temporary and do not lead to significant conflicts.
- *Hyperstress* is a kind of stress that happens when too many tasks and responsibilities pile up on us, and we are unable to adapt to the changes or cope with all that is happening at once.
- *Distress* arises when we don't feel we have control over a situation, or when the source of stress is unclear.

Dealing with change at the workplace, whether you look forward to the change or dread it, will trigger powerful physical and emotional stressors. Nothing is as upsetting to people as change. Nothing has greater potential to cause failures, loss of production, or decreased quality. Yet nothing is as important to the survival of an organization as change. History is full of examples of organizations that failed to change and that are now extinct. The secret to successfully managing change, from the perspective of the employees, is definition and understanding. One can increase a sense of control and direct energies into positive territories when we know how to deal with change.

Resistance to change comes from a fear of the unknown or an expectation of loss. The beginning of an individual's resistance to change is how they perceive the change. The end is how well they are equipped to deal with the change they expect.

Successful organizations will define the change for the employee in as much detail and as early as possible. Providing updates as things develop assists in making the situation clearer. In addition, stakeholders need to understand what is changing and why. Companies also need to understand people's reluctance. Some questions that should be addressed are as follows:

- What will the change be and when it will happen?
- Why is this change happening? And why now?
- Why can't things stay like they have always been?
- Why is it happening to me, or my department?

- What is not changing?
- How will technology and social media platforms change over the next few years?

An individual's degree of resistance to change is determined by whether they perceive the change as good or bad and how severe they expect the impact of the change to be on them. The ultimate acceptance of the change is a function of how much resistance the person has and the quality of their coping skills and their support system.

One of the most baffling problems business executives face is employee resistance to change. Such resistance takes several forms: (1) persistent reduction in output, (2) increase in the number of "quits" and requests for transfer, (3) chronic quarrels, (4) sullen hostility, (5) wildcat strikes, and, of course, (6) the expression of a lot of pseudo-logical reasons why the change will not work. Even the pettier forms of this resistance can be troublesome (Lawrence, 1969).

All too often when supervisors encounter resistance to change, they explain it by quoting the cliché "people resist change" and never look further. Yet changes must continually occur in industry. This applies with force to the all-important "little" changes that constantly take place—changes in work methods, in routine office procedures, in the location of a machine or a desk, in personnel assignments and job titles.

None of these changes makes the headlines, but in total they account for much of our increase in productivity. They are not the spectacular, once-in-a-lifetime technological revolutions that involve mass layoffs or the obsolescence of traditional skills, but they are vital to business progress.

Recognizing that change does happen in organizations and denying that change is or will be occurring only makes things more difficult. Because reactions to organizational change resemble those to the death of a loved one, many studies on change cite the work of psychologist Elisabeth Kübler-Ross (1969), who identified five specific stages of grief—denial and isolation, anger, bargaining, depression, and acceptance.

Organizational communications are always important, but especially so when one faces change. A lack of communication from others can have a negative impact, while effective communication can have a positive one. Part of the fear of change involves dealing with the unknown. This factor can be minimized by talking to others who have undergone such a change.

Change can be frightening and disruptive. However, with the right attitude and actions, you can find opportunities in that change. Clearly, change requires flexibility. The better able one is to adapt to change, the greater the chances of being successful, especially when companies go through reorganization. It is important for the workforce to focus on how they can leverage their existing skills and experiences and become involved in the new adjustments.

Some specific initiatives (Charney, 2006) that organizations can undertake to facilitate smooth transitions to change are to

- involve others in discussions to improve commitment to change;
- communicate reasons for the decisions made;
- when desirable change seems to be slowing or sputtering out, find out why and identify roadblocks that have unexpectedly occurred, and remove them;
- celebrate initiatives that aim to improve performance, whether they succeed or not;
- include change and innovation as core competencies;
- establish measures of self-performance. Ensure that these indicators are also of importance to the stakeholders in the organization;
- get stakeholders involved in setting goals;
- celebrate measurable improvements at periodic get-togethers;
- set up systems to compare and share best practices among different employees in the company;
- communicate openly and freely. Avoid secrecy;
- recognize that not everyone can change equally quickly. Allow for adjustment time and be empathetic with those taking a little longer to adjust to new circumstances;
- provide assistance so workers can master new skills with confidence;
- keep an eye out for people who are acting as roadblocks to change and find out why they are behaving that way. Are their concerns legitimate? If so, respond to them; and
- periodically evaluate readiness for change.

The transition to change may cause feelings of anxiety, hopelessness, and boredom. For most employees work conflicts often causes stress, especially if you are a conflict avoider. When one conflict initiates another, employees often get caught in a destructive conflict which can spiral out of control. Irritability and dismissive behaviors are all common results of stress. It is these results that may lead to other interpersonal conflicts.

Workers who are experiencing stress are less able to participate in conflict resolution because they will have difficulty engaging in higher-level thinking while stressed.

Many organizations have stress management trainings and workshops to assist employees with changes in the corporate structure and the stresses that may accompany those changes. In order to target stress management training an organization may ask employees to complete the following short questionnaire.

In my current position in the company:

I have attended stress management workshops before: Y / N

I would benefit from an overview of stress management strategies.
     (unnecessary) 1   2   3   4   5   (strongly needed)

I need to know what stress management resources are available.
     (unnecessary) 1   2   3   4   5   (strongly needed)

I need to know how to manage my emotions more productively.
     (unnecessary) 1   2   3   4   5   (strongly needed)

I need to know how to employ relaxation techniques.
     (unnecessary) 1   2   3   4   5   (strongly needed)

What additional areas of interest do you have?

List three specific questions that you hope these workshops will be able to answer for you.

Thomas Kuhn (1962) wrote *The Structure of Scientific Revolution* and fathered, defined and popularized the concept of "paradigm shift." He argued that scientific advancement is not evolutionary, but rather is a "series of peaceful interludes punctuated by intellectually violent revolutions," and in those revolutions "one conceptual world view is replaced by another."

The paradigm shift is a change from one way of thinking to another. It's a revolution, a transformation, a type of metamorphosis. It does not just happen, but rather it is driven by agents of change. These agents of change in an organization help to create a paradigm-shift driving change in design, structure, and company policy.

Change is difficult. However, the process has been set in motion and we will co-create our own experience. Kuhn states that "awareness is prerequisite to all acceptable changes of theory." It all begins in the mind of the person. What we perceive is subject to the limitations and distortions produced by our inherited and socially conditional nature. However, we are not restricted by this for we can change. We are moving at an accelerated rate of speed and our state of consciousness is transforming and transcending. Kuhn concludes that "many are awakening as our conscious awareness expands."

Implementing Dynamic Change

Implementing change requires people skills, and the bottom line for most employees will be the question of whether this change will make their organizational lives better or worse. Whatever the kinds of change that people encounter, there are certain patterns of response that occur and re-occur. It is important that change leaders understand some of these patterns, since they are normal outcomes of the change process. Understanding these patterns allows leaders to avoid over-reacting to the behaviors of people who, at times, may be reacting in non-adaptive ways.

Dynamic organizational change may leave employees feeling ill at ease with a laser-focus on what they might have to give up. Some employees might see a marked loss of status or job security. A climate of mistrust could be envisioned by some employees, and some individuals who undergo too much change within too short a time may become dysfunctional and, in some cases, may become physically ill.

In other cases, dynamic change might excite workers to thrive and change their work attitudes and behaviors. Workers perceive that developmental change takes time and effort. Meaningful organizational change does not occur in a climate of mistrust. This trust involves faith in the intentions and behavior of others. Mutual mistrust will doom an otherwise well-conceived change initiative to failure.

When trying to implement dynamic change in an environment where most of the people mistrust each other, success will be limited. Organizations will need to spend some time rebuilding trust if better results are expected from the change effort.

Faulty implementation of organizational change will spell disaster for all stakeholders. People may agree with the change to be implemented, but they may not agree with how these changes will be made. For any significant organizational change effort to be effective, there must be a thoughtful strategy and a thoughtful implementation approach to address any barriers to it.

Most theories of organizational change originated from the work of social psychologist Kurt Lewin (1951). He created a three-stage model of planned change that explained how to initiate, manage, and stabilize the change process. The three stages are unfreezing, changing, and refreezing.

- **Unfreezing**

    Before you can cook a meal that has been frozen, you need to defrost or thaw it. The same can be said of change. Before a change can be implemented, it must go through the initial step of unfreezing. The focus is to create the motivation to change and to develop openness toward something different. To combat resistance to change, the unfreezing stage creates an awareness of how the status quo, or current level of acceptability, is hindering the organization in some way. Old behaviors, ways of thinking, processes, people and organizational structures must all be carefully examined to show employees how necessary a change is for the organization to create or maintain a competitive advantage in the marketplace. This part of the change process has also been referred to as developing the need for change (Lippitt, Watson, and Westerley, 1958).

- **Changing**

    Once the workforce is "unfrozen" they can begin to move, and this is the stage that Lewin recognized as the one where the organization must transition or move into this new state of being. This changing step, also referred to as "movement," is marked by the implementation of the change. Because change involves learning and doing things differently, this stage entails providing the workforce with new data, new models, new procedures, new technologies, and/or new ways of getting the work completed. It's also, consequently, the time that most people struggle with the new reality. Uncertainty and fear may arise, making it the hardest step to overcome and causing resistance to develop. The resistance may be considered a behavior to protect one from the effect of the change (Zander, 1950).

- **Refreezing**

    The final stage of Lewin's change model is freezing, but many refer to it as refreezing to symbolize the act of reinforcing, stabilizing and solidifying the new state after the change. The goal of this stage is to support and reinforce the change. Lewin found the refreezing step to be especially important to ensure that people do not revert to their old ways of thinking or doing prior to the implementation of the change. Efforts must be made to guarantee the change is not lost. Once the new change is exhibited, positive rewards and acknowledgment of individualized efforts are used to reinforce the stability of the change.

Some argue that the refreezing step is outdated in contemporary business due to the continuous need for change. They find it unnecessary to spend time freezing a new state when chances are it will need to be reevaluated and possibly changed again in the immediate future. Without the refreezing step, there is a high chance that people will revert to the old way of doing things. Taking one step forward and two steps back can be a common theme when organizations overlook the refreezing step in anticipation of future change. In some organizations there may be a temptation to move back to behaviors associated with the pre-change state. This process is labeled commitment testing.

Part and parcel of organizational change and development (OD) is the opportunity to perform an impact assessment, which is a formal activity in many organizations. The procedure for performing an impact assessment consists of defining the extent of the proposed change in a manner that is specific and lists all the boundaries. The assessment will furthermore determine the key difference in the changed state compared to a point of reference. The primary focus will be on the possible effects of the key difference and include an examination of any potential or unexpected side effects. Any decision reached needs to identify vulnerabilities with recommendations to mitigate the risks of the decision (Marquis, 2007).

OD consists of planned efforts to help persons work together more effectively, over time, in their organizations. These goals are achieved by applying behavioral science principles, methods and theories adapted from the fields of psychology, sociology, education and management (Hanson & Lubin, 1989). OD is the process of helping organizations improve through change in policies, power, leadership, control or job redesign, and it utilizes a set of interventions that implement planned change aimed at increasing an organization's ability to improve itself. Organizational climate, organizational culture, and organizational strategy are the three main sections of organizational development theory. Change agents, catalysts who help companies deal with old problems in new ways, are used to identify and assist in implementing targeted elements of change. This OD technique is used in Lewin's "changing stage" and in several of Kotter's steps.

The *Johari window* (Luft & Ingham, 1955) is a technique that helps people better understand their relationship with themselves and others. It was created by psychologists Joseph Luft and Harrington Ingham and is used primarily in groups and corporate settings as a problem-solving exercise. It has four sections:

1. *Open/self-area or arena*—Information about the person, his or her attitudes, behavior, emotions, feelings, skills and views, known by the person as well as by others. This is mainly the area where all the communications occur, and the larger the arena becomes, the more effectual and dynamic the relationship will be. In an organization everyone knows what position you hold and the level of importance you hold within the company.
2. *Blind self or blind spot*—Information about you that others in the organization know, but you will be unaware of. Others may interpret you differently than you expect. Coworkers may, at some point, communicate this to you.
3. *Hidden area or façade*—Information that is known to you but will be kept unknown to others. This can be information which you feel reluctant to reveal. This includes feelings, past experiences, fears, etc., that you keep private as it might affect work relationships.
4. *Unknown area*—Information we and others are unaware of. This can be due to negative past work experiences or events which can be unknown for a lifetime. The information will probably remain unknown until there is a discovery of hidden qualities and capabilities or through observation of others. Open workplace communication is also an effective way to decrease the unknown area.

The self in interpersonal communication constitutes the aspects of how we see ourselves, our self-awareness and our self-esteem. These dimensions can play a large role in determining how we act and react in conflict situations. Our self-awareness represents the extent to which we know our strengths and weaknesses, our thoughts and feelings, and our individual personality tendencies. Our *self-esteem* is a measure of how valuable we think we are in the organization.

The Johari window is a useful tool in organizational training which touches upon the areas of self-awareness, personal development, improvement of individual and team communications and group and team dynamics and inter-group relationships.

Teams cannot function effectively without communication and shared information. When perspectives, abilities, and feelings are in the open, team work relationships are dynamic and productive. Individuals can improve the team's success by actively seeking ways to share information within the group and by pushing for transparency, candor, and authenticity. The Johari window is a tool for communicating. Communication can only occur on the common ground found in the arena. The Johari window can assist a team outline and expand the scope of their communication by understanding what already exists as common knowledge and working to bring other important information into the open through discovery, disclosure, and feedback.

Using the Johari Window at the Workplace

My colleague Frank Acuff (2008) is an experienced domestic and international manager who has created the following "skill builder" to assist organizations in achieving its objectives and to focus on maximizing the skills and abilities of its employees.

The following scenario can be viewed or role-played using a fishbowl technique that demonstrates how the four quadrants of the Johari window can be used.

....

Show Me the Money (role-play scenario)

Information Available to the Employee

As a hard-working employee who gets superior performance appraisal ratings, you are about to ask your boss for a 5 percent raise. You received the largest raise in the department—6 percent—three months ago.

Though out-of-cycle increases are virtually unheard of in your organization, you deserve this raise! And besides, the organization's official policy is to "pay for performance," and your boss says that your performance is superior. Now it's time for the boss to say it with money! To replace you would cost the organization a lot more than the 5 percent increase.

Information Available to the Boss

One of your employees has asked to see you about a pay increase. This employee is consistently a superior performer, and you have confirmed this on the employee's performance appraisal forms. This employee received the largest pay increase in the department—6 percent—just three months ago.

The organization's official policy is to "pay for performance." Out-of-cycle increases, however, are virtually unheard of in your organization. These kinds of exceptions set a dangerous precedent and could cause morale problems with the rest of the staff.

....

What would occur during this meeting? What are the areas of disagreement and how do they fit into the four quadrants of the Johari window? What reasoning would the employee use and how would the boss counter? What are several of the possible resolutions that might be agreed to, and which quadrants play a strong role in determining the agreement?

In the scenario "Show Me the Money" the employee asking for a pay increase is using his pay-for-performance argument to justify his request. The organization's response is to deny the request using the argument that the corporate culture does not entertain out-of-cycle increases. Opportunistic employees see opportunities and go for them. For an employee to grab an opportunity they need to know (1) the company culture's model, (2) what the boundaries and limitations are, and (3) the risks involved.

Another view of opportunistic employees is that they are difficult people who present problems. Simple signs of these difficult individuals are easy to recognize: they show up late, leave early, procrastinate, turn their work in late and make excuses for every shortcoming. Such individuals often fail to recognize how their actions contribute to the circumstances for which they might be corrected, disciplined or fired.

From the "open self" in the Johari window we can see that opportunistic members of the workforce might create a harmful and toxic workplace. Some may resent and resist authority and repeatedly challenge those in charge. Dissension might be created among team members with blame for circumstances introduced and bandied about. Of concern to the organization is the possibility that negativity might be generated with customers, vendors, and other companies. Many opportunistic members possess zero enthusiasm for the workplace, colleagues, and projects. They often avoid discussion where their behaviors will be confronted.

Achieving integrative (collaborative) win-win agreements will not usually work with these individuals. If not addressed quickly, continual discord and conflict will linger. Strategic actions must be undertaken to prevent the escalation of conflict to the point it becomes unmanageable. Before a decision is made to let a problematic worker remain or go, it is prudent to consider the many ways that coaching or mentoring can correct and help underperforming or problematic employees. Not every laggard is a lost cause. Affording rehabilitative services could save the organization the cost of hiring and/or training a replacement.

One of the very best ways to uncover, cope with, and correct negative opportunistic employees is to have a company employee handbook that delineates clear policies that will protect the business from toxic influences. It allows the organization to establish crystal clear protocols for dealing with issues and provides a clear path to removing problem employees. It also creates an atmosphere of trust, where the workforce feels secure going to management or the human resources department with concerns.

Finally, the financial impact of toxic employees far exceeds most of our expectations. Over two thousand employees were surveyed (Porath and Pearson, 2009) and their reactions to being victims of workplace toxic behavior are outlined below.

80%	Lost work time worrying about the incident
78%	Felt less commitment to the company
68%	Experienced decline in performance
63%	Lost time avoiding the offender
48%	Decreased their work effort
47%	Decreased their time at work
38%	Performed lower quality work

4

Ethical, Moral and Human Issues in Organizational Conflict

Guidelines, Principles, Codes

An organization is formed when individuals from different backgrounds and varied interests come together for a common platform and work toward predefined goals and objectives. The workforce is the asset of an organization and it is essential for employees to maintain the decorum and culture of the workplace. The way an organization should respond to external environments refers to organizational ethics. Organizational ethics includes various guidelines, principles, and codes of conduct which decide the way individuals should behave at the workplace.

"Businesses can't just say they're ethical, they need to prove they have embedded ethical values," writes Tim Melville-Ross (2013). Businesses have depended upon trust and goodwill for commerce to flourish. Business must be conducted in an open and honest manner; otherwise trust is eroded and businesses fail. However, calls for an increased trust in business miss the point—trust must be earned.

Corporations have entered a new era, the "prove-to-me" era. Trust me and show me are no longer considered good enough. There is a growing demand for businesses not only to say they are ethical, but to prove they have ethical values as part of their organization. Companies that aim high know the benefits of working ethically, but how can they ensure that an ethical culture pervades everything they do? Initiatives such as "investing in integrity" can go some way in measuring a company's actual ethical standards against its own code of ethics, helping to identify whether they are truly living up to their values, from the boardroom down to the staff cafeteria. When trust is eroded, a host of organizational conflicts develop.

From debates over drug testing to analyses of scandals on Wall Street, attention to ethics in business organizations has never been greater, yet much of the attention given to ethics in the workplace overlooks some critical aspects of organizational ethics.

When talking about ethics in organizations, one must be aware that there are two ways of approaching the subject: the *individualistic* approach and the *communal* approach. Each approach incorporates a different view of moral responsibility and a different view of the kinds of ethical principles that should be used to resolve ethical problems.

The development of ethical theory goes back to Plato and Aristotle and the word *ethics* has its roots in the Greek word *ethos*, which translates to conduct, character and customs. Ethics is concerned with the kinds of values and morals an individual or a society finds appropriate. Ethical theory provides a system of rules that guide us in making decisions about what is right or wrong in a situation. Regarding organizations and leadership, ethics is concerned with behaviors, and in any decision-making situation, ethical issues are either implicitly or explicitly involved.

Any adequate understanding of, and effective solution to, ethical problems arising in organizations requires that we take both approaches into account (Brown, 1989). These two approaches, individualistic and communal, also lead to different ways of evaluating moral behavior.

The ethical discussion of issues in the workplace usually takes an individualistic approach, focusing on promoting the good of the individual. Often it highlights individual rights, such as the right to freedom of expression or the right to privacy. This approach chronicles that every individual who is working within the organization is ethically answerable for his or her behavior. The communal approach focuses on the common good and considers harm or benefits to the entire community. It is viewed as a matter of fact that the people who are working together are equally responsible for everything whether they are involved in that task or not because all are considered team members.

When examining ethical and moral issues in an organization, one must clearly understand an organization's culture. Organization culture refers to an organization's beliefs, values, attitudes, ideologies, practices, customs, and language. Even when the beliefs of the organization stem from the chief executive officer or the board of trustees, managers and the workforce need to be committed to the organization's goals for a culture to be shaped. Dimensions that shape an organizational culture (Cartwright & Cooper, 1993) have four definite characteristics: power, bureaucracy, achievement and innovation, and support.

Power: This includes implicit rule, as well as control, stability, and loyalty.
Bureaucracy: Hierarchical structure that includes efficiency, predictability, and control.
Achievement and innovation: Focus on creativity, adaptability, risk taking, and teamwork.
Support: Characteristics include commitment, consensus, and growth.

One of the ethical challenges that large organizations must face is to have a positive impact on the communities where they operate and do business. Walmart's extensive presence has affected communities all over the United States. The first Walmart store opened in 1962 in Rogers, Arkansas, and by 1970 there were 38 stores with sales of $44.2 million. In 1990, Walmart became the country's number one retailer. The organization has faced criticism that its economic impact limits the ability of local businesses to survive. On its website, www.walmartstores.com, it states, "We aim to strengthen local community cohesion and resilience while inspiring our associates to give back. By designing giving programs that meet specific social needs, we work through our stores and associates to enable positive change in the communities we serve."

Ethical discussion considerations for this large organization were developed by Edward C. Brewer (2013).

- Should Walmart be expected to protect small businesses in the communities within which it operates?
- What does it mean for an organization to be ethical in its communications and practices?
- Does Walmart truly harm the downtown areas of small communities, or does it just offer a challenge to change what is uncomfortable for the local merchants?
- Does Walmart's rhetoric communicate a different message than its actions?

Ethical Leadership

Whether in group projects or organizational pursuits, leaders and supervisors engage subordinates and utilize them in their efforts to achieve common goals. Leaders have the ethical responsibility to treat employees with dignity and respect and they must be sensitive to their subordinates' needs and conscientious concerns (Beauchamp & Bowie, 1988).

Ethics is fundamental to leadership and leaders help to establish and reinforce organizational values. The values promoted by company leaders have a significant impact on the values exhibited by the organization (Carlson & Perrewe, 1995), such as the Volkswagen emissions scandal and the controversies surrounding rideshare giant Uber.

These and other examples show what can happen when people at the top of an organization make poor ethical choices and end up in the news or in the courts. There are, however, many other leaders who "raise the bar" and inspire their teams to do the same. In short, ethical leadership is a form of leadership in which individuals demonstrate conduct for the common good that is acceptable and appropriate in every area of their life. It is composed of three major elements: be an example; champion the importance of ethics; and build quality work relationships by communicating.

Ethical leaders define and follow these standards:

- Define the organization's values in clear and succinct words.
- Determine personal values and standards of behavior that align with the organization.
- Create an environment with solid behaviors that others can model.
- Identify ethical dilemmas and the triggers that set them off.
- Prepare in advance to confront and deal with ethical dilemmas while interfacing with individuals in the organizations that provide support and information that assist in the making of correct decisions.

Organizations that endorse ethical leadership have an established policy that states explicitly what actions are acceptable. Possessing a strong moral corporate character isn't enough to inspire leaders to act ethically.

All staff members in leadership positions need to be aware of what is expected of them. Ethical leadership involves holding regular meetings to ensure that everyone is on the same page as well as dealing with conflicting issues that arise in a timely manner. There are many benefits to incorporating an ethics code of conduct including improved communications across the organization's staff, establishing confidence, fairness and stronger customer relationships.

Company structure should ensure that the workforce follows the code of ethics. This can take effort, but the true work of maintaining ethical leadership in the workplace comes down to the choices individuals in management and leadership positions formulate when faced with conflicting values.

Leaders serve as role models for their followers and demonstrate the behavioral boundaries set within an organization. Appropriate and desired behaviors are enhanced through the culture and socialization process of new hires. Employees learn about values from watching leaders in action. The more the leader "talks the talk and walks the walk" by translating internalized values into action, the higher the level of trust and respect he generates from followers.

Values Conflict

People's values are motivational in that they are representations of large goals that apply to all aspects of life. At the workplace many of these values relate job performance and job satisfaction. Organizational conflict can occur when values championed by the company collide with employees' personal values. Some of these values that tend to guide employee behaviors are (1) power, social status and prestige; (2) achievement and personal success; (3) self-direction and independent thought; and (4) security and harmony (Bardi and Schwartz, 2003).

Because values, ethics and morals tend to be stable, individuals are often unwilling to negotiate or compromise with respect to these. Indeed, if the basic substantive issues of the conflict are deeply embedded in the participants' moral orders, these issues are likely to be quite intractable. Mistrust and misunderstanding can lie at the root of conflicts with teammates and other employees. Different values and actions taken by some people to defuse or resolve a conflict may often be perceived as threatening by the other party. Misunderstandings and erroneous perceptions may arise because individuals often perceive, define, and deal with conflict in different ways.

To distinguish between one's interests and fundamental values is important. There are many cases where conflict results from a clash between differing worldviews. If individuals or work teams have radically different ideas about the best way to work on a project, they are likely to stress the importance of very different things. When the basic substantive issues of a conflict are embedded in a team's moral views, these issues are likely to be intractable. Any attempts by conflict managers to resolve such conflicts solely by addressing interests are likely to prove ineffective.

Intellectual Capital

What is intellectual capital? In *The Wealth of Knowledge*, Thomas A. Stewart (2001) states, "Simply put, knowledge assets are talent, skills, know-how, know-what and relationships—and the machines and networks that embody them—that can be used to create wealth." He further notes, "Because knowledge has become the single most important factor of production, managing intellectual assets has become the single most important task of business."

For today's organization an important consideration is the ability to understand the nature of and realize the value of the assets of their workforce or intellectual capital. This is the intangible value of a business, covering its employees and the value inherent in its relationship with them. Business ethics has a positive impact on the development of intellectual capital. Knowledge has become the most important asset of modern businesses, and, clearly, business ethics is associated with the development of intangible knowledge resources, intellectual capital. Organizations with ethical values at their core reinforce ethical conduct and successfully build trust with their stakeholders, leading to the formation of an ethical and trustworthy corporate culture and a positive corporate environment.

It is becoming accepted by an increasing number of companies that future success depends upon their ability to utilize their intellectual resources and to appreciate the inherent value of these. However, many organizations spend less time and effort in evaluating and tracking these than they do financial and physical assets (Cattell, 2005).

A business guided by ethical values reinforces ethical conduct and gains the trust of stakeholders such as employees, customers and suppliers. Influences of ethical values and trust in them form an organizational culture of ethicality and trustworthiness and generate a positive environment that encourages employees' open communication, knowledge sharing, cooperation and creativity and better organizational problem solving and learning, leading to enhanced organizational capital (Su, 2014).

Business ethics received worldwide attention from the scandals of globally renowned corporations such as Enron and Worldcom. Although unethical behaviors may generate short-term benefits, ethics can bring to businesses competition and better performance through attracting talent, strengthening employee commitment, and enhancing their image in the minds of investors, customers and suppliers. Current successful and thriving organizations are those that create intellectual capital and convert it into applicable methods to improve their activities and performance. In addition, an ethical climate is the key issue for such organizations gaining success in implementing the relevant supportive systems.

Conflict Management Styles

The management of conflict is the ability to identify and handle conflicts sensibly, fairly, and efficiently. Since conflicts in a business are a natural part of the workplace, it is important that there are people who understand conflicts and know how to resolve them. In today's market it is prudent for an organization to employ conflict resolvers.

When conflict happens, managers, mediators, and conflict resolution specialists need to respond quickly to reach resolution. As mentioned earlier, Kilmann and Thomas (1974) identified the five styles that managers could follow: accommodating, avoiding, collaborating, competing, and compromising. These five styles have shown to be a standard set of concepts for understanding conflict.

The individual or department tasked with resolving organizational conflict will use a style that is consistent with their own orientation to conflict. Three styles of conflict management personalities (Filley, 1975) are described below.

1. *The tough battler:* conveys strategies that indicate determination to make small concessions to reach tough, but fair, agreements.
2. *The friendly helper:* a flexible approach to compel the disputants to express understanding for the other side's issues and concerns.
3. *The problem solver:* the primary emphasis on satisfying each party's issues and concerns.

Clearly, self-management of conflict is the optimal norm; however, when organizations need to resolve workplace conflict, they will have to select a conflict style that will get the job done. Each party to the dispute, whether they are individual employees, a work team, or an entire department, will have different views and approaches to the main issue in dispute as well as other sub-issues. Dealing with major and minor differences in a conflict will necessitate that the organization thoroughly understand the areas of incompatibility (Folger, Poole and Stutman, 2013). The conflict session begins with having a preliminary understanding of all the issues, interests, and positions. Next is addressing the legitimacy of those issues, interests and positions and a realization that the differences cannot be resolved without working together. All sides need to have motivation to resolve the conflict, even if the motivation is only knowledge that the other side will continue to resist and prolong the conflict unless a mutually acceptable resolution is achieved.

Undertaking the resolution of workplace conflict involves skilled individuals at the company that have been trained in a rigorous conflict resolution, negotiation and mediation program. Questions that need to be addressed include (1) Do the solutions meet everyone's needs? (2) Has all appropriate information been gathered with channels of communication open? (3) Are deadlocks and impasses resolved in a fair way utilizing caucusing and time-outs? (4) Is the resolution a win-win for both sides? (5) Are different cultures, values, assumptions, and beliefs taken into consideration that could affect the conflict in question?

The following scenario can be viewed or role-played using a fishbowl technique that demonstrates how various problem-solving conflict styles can be used involving an internal company conflict.

....

I Can't Get No Satisfaction

Information Available to the VP of Information Technology

You are the VP of the Department of Information Technology, and you have been asked to meet with a Project Manager for a company-wide initiative. This new project is a Customer Feelings and Satisfaction Survey which has the full support of the COO. This project involves the design of a customer survey that will appear on the company website that will gather information and sentiments of customers and users of the company's full product line.

The PM wants Matthew Smart to lead this project for the next 10 months. Matthew has been in your department for nine years and he is your "best" employee. You really do not want to give him up, but you will need to appear cooperative.

Information for the Project Manager

As the Project Manager for the creation of a company Customer Feelings and Satisfaction Survey, you have decided to meet with the VP of the Department of Information Technology to request the participation of Matthew Smart. You will need his participation for 10–14 hours per month for the next 10 months.

102   4. Ethical, Moral and Human Issues in Organizational Conflict

> You understand that Matthew has been with the company for nine years and that the VP might be reluctant to let him participate, but you think you might have some leverage because the COO is strongly in favor of this project.

....

What would occur during this meeting? What are the areas of disagreement and how do they fit into the five styles of conflict management? What conflict styles might be adopted by the PM and the VP and how would they affect the discussion? If several of the conflict styles merged together, what would the impact be? What are several of the possible resolutions that might be agreed to? How would power and leverage play into this internal company conflict?

Individual Profile Styles

Assessing one's personal behavior in conflict situations can help individuals, teams, divisions and the entire organization better understand themselves and assist in adapting behaviors to focus on commonalities and improve working relationships. People in all companies have different styles. One's thinking style or communication style might conflict with somebody else's thinking style or communication style. Sometimes conflict issues revolve around values. The challenge is that values are deeply held and adapting to styles is one thing, but dealing with conflicting values is another.

A deep analysis of one's communication style can increase self-knowledge and conflict response, and it can also motivate people to reduce stress and solve problems. Four communication styles all approach conflict in different ways (Payne, 2001).

- *Direct*: Has a strong need to control people and situations. Emphasis is on overcoming opposition and trying to win. They take authority to resolve differences and make quick decisions about what needs to be done.
- *Avoidance*: Has a tendency toward passivity and withdrawal. Tend to sidestep conflict issues while suppressing their own needs and feelings.
- *Collaborative*: Uses a proactive approach to work with others to find solutions that satisfy the concerns of all the stakeholders. Help others to verbalize their issues and concerns.

- *Accommodate*: Has a desire to maintain harmonious relationships while cooperating readily. Often neglect their own personal concerns in favor of satisfying the concerns of others.

See Kilmann-Thomas Conflict Mode Instrument for additional styles.

Motivations

Motivation is generally defined as the force that compels us to action. It propels us to work hard and induces us to succeed. Motivation influences our behavior and our ability to accomplish goals. Are the motivations that move employees the same as those that move senior management? Do individuals share an understanding of how ambitions and fears influence the day-to-day functioning of the company? Does the organization have transformative agendas that drive projects, product development, and services forward? Of the time spent looking forward, is there a distinct and collective view of the future?

Motivation is the desire to do things. It's the difference between waking early to work on a project and delaying until the last moment to get moving! It's the central element in setting and attaining goals.

Different needs motivate people differently. Building healthy and successful teams, departments and divisions is not easy. There are several basic needs and many in the workforce are motivated by (1) affiliation, the need to belong where workers find the social aspects of the environment important; (2) power, the ability to gain satisfaction from being in control and/or having influence; (3) esteem, gaining praise and recognition; (4) achievement, self-motivation to derive satisfaction from task accomplishments; and (5) freedom, the autonomy and independence to select one's own options.

Building successful teams is easier when there's recognition of what keeps people motivated. Creating a work environment that supports people's needs goes a long way toward building a productive workforce. Some researchers have found that perceived self-interest, meaning the rewards one believes to be at stake, is the most significant factor in predicting dedication and satisfaction toward work. It can account for about 75 percent of personal motivation toward accomplishment. For more complex tasks people may be more motivated by the need for autonomy, mastery and purpose (Pink, 2011).

Motivation is one of the forces that lead to performance. When we one "right" way to deal with differences. They go on to state that "when a manager's subordinates become involved in a heated disagreement, they do not tend to proceed in a systematic manner to resolve their difference. The issues often remain unclear to them, and they may talk *at* rather than *to* one another."

In analyzing the major issues of the disagreement, the resolution specialist should look for the following:

- *Targets.* Sometimes the disagreement is about what should be accomplished, the desirable objectives of a department, division, or specific position within the organization.
- *Data.* Sometimes the disagreement occurs because individuals have different definitions of a problem, are keen to different segments of relevant information, accept or reject different information as factual, or have differing impressions of their respective authority.
- *Approaches.* Sometimes individuals differ about the procedures or strategies which would most likely achieve a mutually desired goal.
- *Tenets.* Sometimes the disagreement is over ethics, the way power should be exercised, or moral considerations. Such differences may affect the choice of either goals or methods.

A large area of organizational disagreements involves the management of generational differences in the workplace. Different generations possess various qualities and have differing needs in the workplace. There probably isn't a company in the United States that isn't grappling with the problem of managing different generations. Problems can arise from differing mindsets and communication styles of workers born in different eras. The frictions may be aggravated by new technology and work patterns that mix workers of different ages in ever-changing teams.

The *Traditionalist Generation*, born between 1925 and 1945, grew up with many rules and pressures to conform to and many are now retired; however, some continue to work as executives and members of boards of directors. *Baby Boomers*, born between 1946 and 1964, are usually competitive and think workers should pay their dues. *Gen Xers*, born between 1965 and 1980, are more likely to be skeptical and independent-minded. *Millennials*, born in 1981 or later, usually enjoy teamwork, feedback and technology. Accommodating different learning and work styles are the keys to avoiding conflict.

Strategies that organizations can use to minimize generational conflicts are to focus on goals and set clear expectations. Minimizing these conflicts can be accomplished by (1) facilitating mentoring; (2) keeping employees engaged; (3) encouraging a balance between work and personal life; (4) creating simple recognition programs; and (5) accommodating employees' personal needs and giving employees a voice to make suggestions.

Since workers from different generations have always worked together, why does this situation currently appear to be raising challenges for human resource management? Different generations are said to have different values and expectations regarding work which are not easily compatible. People from different generations are working together for longer periods now than they did in the past. Workers are less likely to follow the clear-cut work-to-retirement path that was formerly standard. People leave their jobs, upgrade their skills, look for new jobs, change careers, retire and then, increasingly, re-enter the labor market. The difficulties stemming from this situation are brought about by discrepancies in the management practices of companies themselves. Stable, high-quality jobs are becoming scarce (Saba, 2013).

Effective teams should value different views, encourage active listening, decrease ambiguity among team members' roles, support the sharing of expertise, share recognition and appreciation, value hard work and build in humor and levity in their work sessions.

Group Thinking

Groupthink in an organization occurs when a team, group or division with a particular agenda makes irrational or problematic decisions because its members value harmony and coherence over accurate analysis and critical evaluation. When people are so committed to the agenda, they fail to engage in conflict over differing ideas when they should. Individual members of the group are strongly discouraged from any disagreement with the consensus and set aside their own thoughts and feelings to unquestioningly follow the word of the leader and other group members.

In a groupthink situation, group members refrain from expressing

4. Ethical, Moral and Human Issues in Organizational Conflict

doubts, judgments or disagreement with the consensus and ignore any ethical or moral consequences of any group decision that furthers their cause. When a team is too cohesive, and members do not speak out, there is no risk-taking, creativity or independent thinking. Irving Janis (1972) documented eight symptoms of groupthink.

1. *Illusion of invulnerability*—Creates excessive optimism that encourages taking extreme risks.
2. *Collective rationalization*—Members discount warnings and do not reconsider their assumptions.
3. *Belief in inherent morality*—Members believe in the rightness of their cause and therefore ignore the ethical or moral consequences of their decisions.
4. *Stereotyped views of out-groups*—Negative views of "enemy" make effective responses to conflict seem unnecessary.
5. *Direct pressure on dissenters*—Members are under pressure not to express arguments against any of the group's views.
6. *Self-censorship*—Doubts and deviations from the perceived group consensus are not expressed.
7. *Illusion of unanimity*—The majority view and judgments are assumed to be unanimous.
8. *Self-appointed "mindguards"*—Members protect the group and the leader from information that is problematic or contradictory to the group's cohesiveness, view, and/or decisions.

The *Abilene Paradox*, a term coined by Jerry B. Harvey in 1974 (1988), is the inability to manage agreement, not conflict. Harvey named the paradox after a trip his family made to Abilene, Texas. Harvey's father-in-law was concerned that his family was growing bored sitting at home, so he suggested a trip to Abilene for dinner. Despite no real interest in making the hour-long trip on a hot summer afternoon, all enthusiastically agreed to the journey. Harvey recognized that this false agreement is all too common in group decision-making and called the phenomenon the Abilene Paradox.

The following symptoms are said to exist in organizations that tend to fall for the paradox:

- Organization members agree privately, as individuals, as to the nature of the situation or problem facing the organization.

- Organization members agree privately, as individuals, as to the steps that would be required to cope with the situation or problem they face.
- Organization members fail to accurately communicate their desires and/or beliefs to one another. In fact, they do just the opposite and thereby lead one another into misperceiving the collective reality.
- With such invalid and inaccurate information, organization members make collective decisions that lead them to take actions contrary to what they want to do, and thereby arrive at results that are counterproductive to the organization's intent and purposes.
- Because of taking actions that are counterproductive, organization members experience frustration, anger, irritation, and dissatisfaction with their organization. Consequently, they form subgroups with trusted acquaintances and blame other subgroups for the organization's dilemma.
- Finally, if organization members do not deal with the generic issue—the inability to manage agreement—the cycle repeats itself with greater intensity.

When an organization makes decisions, the Abilene Paradox occurs because people experience anxiety over selecting a specific course of action. There is trepidation of being separated from the team. Conflict ensues when members exhibit different opinions in the group as opposed to one on one. Employees are discouraged to dissent, and this is often seen as a lack of commitment. When an individual on a team offers constructive criticism, even if it is encouraged, they might be accused of failing to be a team player. Anxiety and frustration can cause workers to avoid responsibility or even attempt to blame others. This can result in a lack of trust. Many things erode trust. Employees distrust management that doesn't listen to their concerns and that delegates not only tasks but also blame for failed initiatives. Corporate politics then lead to backstabbing and blame-shifting among employees under such management, as everyone does what they can to avoid being targeted.

A real-life example of the Abilene Paradox involves a group of friends planning to celebrate and treat a group member on her birthday. One person suggests the moderately expensive Harlen's Steakhouse. No one really likes the choice or wants to go. No one speaks up and no one wants to appear cheap, so that is where the birthday celebration takes place. This poor communication can be mitigated by having even one individual speak up. The risk for the person who frequently speaks up is that they could be seen as uncooperative and a spoil-sport. It is highly likely that today there will be people who speak up. This may be due, in part, to generational differences.

Generational Differences

When we talk about generational differences, it's easy to fall into overly generalized stereotypes. Stereotypes are trivial for many reasons; the key one is how quickly they can change given history and context. No generation is one monolithic group of people who all behave the same way. It's important to consider what makes each one tick because this is the first time in history that different distinct generations are in the workplace simultaneously. Having five generations side by side in society is nothing new. Thinking about what drives each generation with which we interact can provide insight to how to maintain harmonious relations and how to avoid and/or confront conflict. Each person in the workforce is a unique individual, but these generational signifiers may offer some clues into the behavior of people born in different eras.

The West Midland Family Center (2018) developed a "generational differences chart" which includes the attributes of each generation.

Traditionalists (1928–1945)

Committed to company	Linear work style
Competent	Loyal to organization/employers
Confident	Organized
Conservative	Patriotic
Dedication	Respectful of authority
Doing more with less	Rules of conduct
Ethical	Sacrifice
Fiscally prudent	Strong work ethic
Hard-working	Task oriented
Historical viewpoint	Thrifty—abhor waste
Honor	Trust hierarchy and authority

Baby Boomers (1946–1964)

- Ability to handle a crisis
- Ambitious
- Anti-establishments
- Challenge authority
- Competent
- Competitive
- Consensus leadership
- Consumerism
- Ethical
- Good communication skills
- Idealism
- Live to work
- Loyal to careers and employers
- Most educated as compared to other three generations
- Multi-taskers
- Optimistic
- Political correctness
- Strong work ethic
- Rebellious against convention, like their conservative parents
- Traditionally found their worth in their work ethic but now seek a healthy life/work balance
- Willing to take on responsibility

Generation X (1965–1980)

- Adaptable
- Angry but don't know why
- Antiestablishment mentality
- Big gap with Boomers
- Can change
- Crave independence
- Confident
- Competent
- Ethical
- Flexible
- Focus on result
- Free agent
- Highest number of divorced parents
- High degree of brand loyalty
- Ignore leadership
- Independent
- Loyal to manager
- Pampered by their parents
- Pragmatic
- Results driven
- Self-starters
- Self sufficient
- Skeptical of institutions
- Strong sense of entitlement
- Unimpressed with authority
- Willing to take on responsibility
- Willing to put in the extra time to get the job done
- Work/life balance

Millennials (1981–1996)

- Ambitious but not entirely focused
- At ease in teams
- Attached to their gadgets and parents
- Best educated—confident
- Diversity focused—multiculturalism
- Eager to spend money
- Fiercely independent
- Focus is children/family
- Focus on change using technology
- Friendly scheduled, structured lives
- Globalism (global way of thinking)
- Greatly indulged by fun-loving parents
- Have not lived without computers
- Heroism—consider parents their heroes
- High speed stimulus junkies
- Hope to make life contributions to world
- Incorporate individual resp. into their jobs
- Innovative—think out of box
- Individualistic yet group-oriented
- Invited as children to play a lead role in family's purchasing and travel decisions
- Look to the workplace for direction and to help them achieve their goals
- Loyal to peers
- Most doted upon of any generation
- Net-centric team players
- Open to new ideas
- Optimistic
- Parent advocacy (Parents are advocates)
- Political savvy (like the Boomers)
- Respect given for competency not title
- Respectful of character development
- Seek responsibility early on in their roles
- Self-absorbed
- Sociable—makes workplace friends
- Strong sense of entitlement
- Techno savvy—Digital generation
- Think mature generation is "cool"
- Very patriotic (shaped by 9/11)
- Want to please others

Gen-Z (1997–)

Eager to communicate face to face	Have a great deal in common with Millennials
Enjoy working alone	Highly competitive
Focus on recent technology	Prone to multitask
Lean toward job security	Recently entering the workplace

Organizations that understand how to address generational conflicts successfully and leverage each generation's strengths will be better able to keep employees motivated and productive.

The following discussion can take place in small groups that can demonstrate how different generational types can reach decisions about this downsizing exercise.

....

Downsizing (group discussion)

You are a member of a task force that has been asked to oversee the downsizing of a department. There are 10 individuals in the department and jobs for only six people. These six people will be reassigned to other groups and the remaining four will be out of work. Try to reach consensus on the six who will be offered new jobs. The 10 people in the department are as follows.

a. A 39-year-old divorced woman who has reentered the workplace two years ago, after raising three children.
b. A 31-year-old engineer who is known to be a confirmed racist.
c. A former priest who left the church under questionable circumstances, but who is performing very well on the job.
d. A 19-year-old woman who is putting herself through college.
e. A 57-year-old white male whose wife is dying of cancer.
f. An opinionated woman who has a strong track record and has been lobbying for promotion.
g. A 26-year-old man who is a strident conservative Republican.
h. A woman who works two jobs to support her invalid parents.
i. A man who was formerly a member of the terror group ISIS and now works with the CIA to destroy them.
j. A talented man with several years of excellent service who is a homosexual.

Using the attributes chart, examine the responses of each generational type as it relates to the age of the members of the department, gender, family background, marital status, political affiliation, sexual orientation, and social affiliations.

....

The management of differences, no matter which generational camp one fits into, focuses on agreement. Agreement on aims is an appropriate starting point. Common wisdom suggests that clarity about aims leads to success in working with people regardless of organizational policies. Organizations often struggle to reach agreements because they bring together people, departments and divisions that have different resources and expertise.

A New Mindset

Companies will have to change the way they deal with the next generation of new employees. Every generation has been exposed to a unique set of events that defines their place in history and molds their outlook. This new generation has grown up with such defining moments as the school shootings in Columbine High School in Littleton, Colorado, and Stoneman Douglas High School in Parkland, Florida, the Gulf War, the #MeTooMovement, the terrorist attacks of September 11, 2001, devastating hurricanes, the BP oil disaster, and the Trump presidency. Certainly, the most significant change affecting the new young workforce lies in the computer, the Internet and other technologies (Tapscott, 2009).

For the new mindset to function, and succeed in the workforce, organizations must rethink and adapt to the ways of the new generation's culture. Don Tapscott has postulated these guidelines:

1. Rethink the focus of talent management.
2. Do not recruit, initiate relationships.
3. Do not train, engage. Employment is a relationship and a two-way street.
4. Rethink authentic authority.
5. Do not supervise, but instead build next generation collaborative work systems.
6. Do not retain employees. Evolve lasting relationships.
7. Listen to the workforce when designing work spaces, processes, management systems, and collaborative working models.

The new generation focuses on the activity, not the specific technology, that enables them accomplish tasks. It's not text messaging, instant messaging and e-mailing. It's communicating, collaborating and engaging. Organizations that understand this will revolutionize the workplace of tomorrow. Working with these recent hires is about developing new opportunities and increasing profits and successes. The new generation is the largest in American history, over 100 million and counting, and its intuitive use of technology is quickly changing how workplaces work.

Reaction to Crises and Catastrophes

Several years ago, I designed and taught a crisis management course at the Graduate School of Education at Pace University in New York City. The curriculum included

- understanding and analyzing the challenge of safe environments;
- developing perspectives on safe workplaces;
- formulating characteristics of organizations that are safe/responsive to stakeholders;
- defining the role of leaders as a risk manager;
- developing community collaborations;
- defining and analyzing what a crisis is and planning appropriate responses;
- conducting needs assessments to design an action-planning checklist;
- collaborating to build the emergency management response team;
- exploring crisis prevention initiatives;
- creating guiding principles for effective facilitation;
- evaluating the conflict resolution principles of negotiation and mediation; and
- defining proactive roles of all stakeholders.

Crises occur in a variety of settings, schools as well as organizations, for a variety of reasons. In the United States, we have, unfortunately, become accustomed to dealing with crises involving mass shootings. These horrific acts capture our attention because of the nature of the crisis, the media coverage, and the community response. Conflicts in such places as Littleton, Colorado, Virginia Tech, the Washington Navy Yard, Pittsburgh's Tree of Life synagogue, and Sutherland Springs Church deserve our attention, but we must also be cognizant of the many, many other "small" crises that develop each day in our communities and companies. I am reminded of my visit to a high school in New York City that installed airport-like metal detectors to deter violence and conflicts involving weapons. I was taken aback when a sophomore mentioned that "those metal detectors can't detect the hate in my heart!"

Situations like separating children from parents as they cross U.S. borders, Hurricane Maria in Puerto Rico, and the California wildfires, although creating traumatic characteristics, in and of themselves, do not constitute crisis. These events trigger crises. The three essential elements that must be present for a situation to be considered a crisis are (1) a precipitating event, (2) a perception of the event that leads to subjective distress, and (3) diminished functioning when the distress is not alleviated by customary coping strategies (Puleo and McGlothlin, 2010).

Shootings, hurricanes, earthquakes, floods, and wildfires define crises that demand attention and intervention. Crises in organizations are markedly different. On April 20, 2010, the oil drilling rig *Deepwater Horizon*, operating in the Macondo Prospect in the Gulf of Mexico, exploded and sank, resulting in the deaths of 11 workers and the largest spill of oil in the history of marine oil drilling operations. Over four million barrels of oil flowed from the damaged well over an 87-day period before it was finally capped on July 15, 2010. The United States filed a complaint in district court against British Petroleum Exploration & Production and several other defendants alleged to be responsible for the spill. The explosion of the oil rig badly damaged the company's reputation and has cost it tens of billions of dollars in fines and settlements. In response to this issue British Petroleum took the following significant measures to manage recovery:

1. Over 30 spill response vessels including a large storage barge.
2. Skimming capacity of more than 171,000 barrels per day.
3. Offshore storage capacity of 122,000 barrels and an additional 175,000 barrels available and on standby.
4. Supplies of more than 100,000 gallons of dispersants and four aircraft ready to spray dispersant to the spill, and the pre-approval of the U.S. Coast Guard to use them.
5. Pre-planned forecasting of 48-hour spill trajectory which indicates spilled oil will remain well offshore during that period.
6. Pre-planned staging of resources for protection of environmentally sensitive areas.

In the years that followed the *Deepwater Horizon* crisis the fury and outcry over BP's role in the spill effectively erased the progress BP had made on the corporate responsibility fronts in the previous decade. Long before

Without a doubt, most workplace violence spotlights issues of relationship violence. Three distinct areas of relationship violence are (1) verbal abuse, (2) emotional abuse, and (3) physical abuse. The perpetrator of relationship violence usually does not have ties to the business but has a personal relationship with the intended victim. This type of violence can occur in all workplaces but is most difficult to prevent in workplaces that are accessible to the public during business hours, such as retail businesses, and/or have only one location, making it impossible to transfer employees who are being threatened. Women are at higher risk of being victims of this type of violence than men.

The responses to these types of relationship violence are (1) looking for fairness in reaching resolutions, (2) honest communication, (3) mutual affirmation and respect, and (4) responsibility and accountability. One way to minimize relationship violence is networking to expand areas of expertise, assistance and securing information that covers a wide variety of problems that need to be addressed. Many times, HR is helpful in this regard.

Every organization needs to address workplace violence. Risks of violence increase during times of extreme job stress. Understaffed job sites, overworked employees and times of downsizing can create a tense and potentially dangerous context for the development of violent behavior (Jackson-Cherry and Erford, 2010). Supervisors and safety professionals at every workplace should develop a policy on violence that includes employee training, mock training exercises and drills and the adoption of a zero-tolerance policy toward workplace violence.

One of the most high-profile incidents of workplace violence occurred at a San Francisco United Parcel Service warehouse facility in June of 2017. Just before 9:00 a.m. local time, a driver in full uniform opened fire on his coworkers, killing three and injuring five. When police arrived on the scene, he turned the gun on himself. Although no definitive motive has been agreed upon, the perpetrator apparently felt disrespected by his fellow employees, which could have led to the violent outburst. Employees who were interviewed later stated how surprised they were; the man never displayed any prior violent tendencies.

Nothing can guarantee that an employee will not become a victim of workplace violence. Organizations can institute training workshops and programs that teach the workforce to recognize, avoid or defuse potentially violent situations. Having strong workplace violence policies are important for every organization. Proper policies and procedures allow businesses to minimize the impact of incidents that nobody sees coming.

Crisis Prevention and Management

Crisis prevention is a difficult task, but what is abundantly clear is that the basic crisis prevention process is to identify crisis threat or warning signs and take actions that will reduce the likelihood of that risk becoming a crisis (Coombs, 2012).

The concept of crisis prevention, intervention, and management includes all of the following elements: confronting a momentous decision, encountering the pivotal moment, and facing both peril and promise. Crisis management is the rapid collaboration of a team to assist people and/or the organization in surviving a crisis, resolving it positively, and moving forward. Most people successfully handle traumatic or crisis events and even achieve personal growth by dealing with these adversities. Using Salikeu's (1990) application of Lazarus' (1981) perspective, the BASICS model of the crisis experience is as follows:

Behavioral—what people do
Affective—how people feel
Somatic—how people respond physically
Interpersonal—how people relate to others
Cognitive—how people think
Spiritual—what people believe and value

Today's organizations must contend with reactions to new types of crisis and trauma. Despite considerable social, community, law enforcement and organizational changes, most companies do not receive specific training in responding to the diversity of crisis situations. Specific events include, but are not limited to, the following:

- accidents involving employees;
- suicides or homicides at the workplace;
- assaults on employees or other workforce members;
- hostage situations on company grounds;
- terrorist activities;
- fire or chemical spills;
- natural disasters;
- confrontations between company employees;
- technological problems (breakdowns, hacks, corrupted software); and
- management misconduct (acts of illegality).

Crisis Management Team

A crisis management team (CMT) is formed to protect an organization against the adverse effects of crisis. Crisis management teams prepare an organization for inevitable threats and are formed to decide on future courses of action and to devise strategies to help organizations come out of difficult times as soon as possible. The five major roles of such teams are to focus on

1. detecting the early signs of crisis;
2. identifying the problem area(s);
3. conferring with employees, face to face, and discussing the identified areas of concern;
4. preparing crisis management plans that work best during emergency situations; and
5. help the organization come out of difficult times and prepare it for the future.

Most organizations have a crisis management plan in the event of a fire. Individuals are selected as wardens, and people know about extinguishers, escape routes and shelter. Procedures are also set into motion to notify the fire department and law enforcement. Most organizations have sporadic drills to practice these plans and behaviors. A crisis management team should include (1) department heads, (2) the chief executive officer and people closely associated with him or her, (3) security personnel, (4) human resource representatives, (5) board of directors, and (6) media advisors. When the crisis demands it, trauma and grief counselors should be available. CMTs that lack expertise in any of these crisis areas can reach out to the American Academy of Experts in Traumatic Stress which demonstrates a commitment to the advancement of intervention for survivors of traumatic events. It is the first step in a process aimed at identifying expertise among professionals across disciplines. The academy works in collaboration with its sister organization, the National Center for Crisis Management.

As part of a proactive response to organizational crises, the CMT might already exist, but may not be sufficiently "wide" or "deep" (Lewis, 2006). Lewis states that, in times of crisis, organizations need leadership and management at all levels to work together. There must be established roles and goals for each CMT member and there must be visibility and availability of the team leader(s).

The primary role of the CMT is to analyze the situation and formulate crisis management plans to save the organization's reputation and standing in the industry. A team leader is appointed to take charge of the situation immediately and encourage the employees to work as a single unit. One of the major roles of the CMT is to stay in touch with external clients as well as media. The team must handle critical situations well.

Planning is essential to the adoption of a step-by-step approach during critical situations. Becoming excited and nervous does not solve any problem; instead it makes the situation worse. Any plan prepared by superiors, members of CMT and related employees helps the organization overcome a crisis in the best possible way.

A crisis management plan (CMP) refers to a detailed plan that describes the various actions that need to be taken during critical situations or crises. This CMP helps all stakeholders to adopt a focused approach during emergency situations because it provides a comprehensive overview of the roles and responsibilities of employees during crisis. Finally, the CMP protects an organization from inevitable threats and reduces instability and uncertainty among the employees and helps them focus on their work. During times of crisis, we are quick to address physical trauma. We don't wait to call for help and emergency medical personnel. Unfortunately, a hidden trauma may often be ignored. This trauma leaves the deepest scars and changes people forever—traumatic stress (Lerner and Shelton, 1999).

Many lessons were learned after September 11, 2001. One of them was that crises do not always have a beginning and an end, and that traumatic stress can impact individuals, groups, organizations, communities, and even an entire nation. We have all observed how traumatic stress disables people, causes disease, precipitates mental disorders, leads to substance abuse, and destroys relationships and families.

Drs. Lerner and Shelton explain that traumatic stress has many "faces" and is experienced during and in the aftermath of crisis (e.g., facing a serious illness, dealing with the loss of a coworker, experiencing an accident, etc.). Their book provides valuable information, offering practical strategies, to help people during a traumatic event. This is a time when people are perhaps most suggestible and vulnerable to traumatic stress and is a tremendous opportunity for intervention.

Organization's Crisis Plan

Self-assessment, management and delivery of crisis plans are important for organizations. Crises take cognitive and emotional tolls on all involved and periodic assessments are good indicators of successful crisis management and can also be indicators of lacking or reduced functioning. Questions used to assess an organization's crisis and continuity plan (Lewis, 2006) include the following:

1. What is the crisis committee called?
2. Who are the members?
3. Who is the "head" of the team or committee?
4. How often does the team meet?
5. Where is the plan kept?
6. How is the plan been communicated to supervisors and the workforce?
7. Are there drills? How often? Announced or unannounced?

Early emergency and crisis preparedness and effective responses by an organization can result in interventions that help both stakeholders and the company heal and recover. The fundamental components of the CMT and the CMP are established to address specific crisis problems. A comprehensive approach to crisis management is the coordination and collaboration of all individuals to minimize, resolve and address major issues that arise. Effective crisis response strategies should address the following concepts: stress management, trauma, adaptation, coping skills, and resiliency.

5

Workplace Collaborations

Advantages of Collaboration

Collaborative work teams are among the most popular workplace innovations since the 1980s. MIT economist Paul Osterman (1994) found that more than half the companies he surveyed were using teams to accomplish work and that 40 percent of those companies had most of their employees working in teams. Organizations divide the emphasis of their work into groups, divisions, departments and teams. These gatherings of people are more than just a collection of individuals. They exist for sharing a goal or project and seeing it through to fruition. Their collaboration is based on collectively communicating within the team structure to create coordinated interactions to accomplish the task at hand (Forsyth, 1999). That denotes the key feature of workplace collaboration: all individuals work together on a common project for which they are all accountable.

With increasing competition, it has become important to encourage creativity in the office, to improve productivity and to promote healthy employee relationships. Working in teams enables employees to be speedier and more effective in their work as compared to individuals who work on projects on their own. The characteristics of a group were outlined by Johnson and Johnson (1997).

Characteristics of a Group

Goal Orientation	People joining together for some purpose, and to achieve some goal.
Interdependent	People who have some type of relationship, see connections among themselves or believe that share a common purpose.

Interpersonal Interaction	People who communicate and interact with one another.
Perception of Membership	Recognition that there is a collective to which one belongs.
Structured Relations	Roles, rule, and norms that control people's interactions.
Mutual Influence	Impact people have on one another because of their connections.
Individual Motivation	Satisfaction of personal needs through membership in the group.

Successful collaboration takes place when two individuals or a group of people work together toward achieving a common goal by sharing their ideas and skills. Collaboration allows for acknowledgment of each other's work styles and communication behaviors and eliminates situations of avoidance and competition. This can happen in traditional as well as virtual teams (teleconferencing, video-conferencing and cloud-based programs).

When employees work together on projects, they become involved with the concerns of their teammates and aim to find mutually satisfying solutions to the task(s) at hand. Mutual understanding is the key to successful collaboration efforts. Here are some of the key advantages of collaboration (Daniels and Walker, 2001).

- Collaboration is much less competitive.
- It highlights mutual learning and fact-finding.
- It allows for exploration of differences in underlying values.
- The conclusions are arrived at by the individuals through an interactive and reflexive process.
- It has the potential to build capacities in areas like conflict management and decision-making.

Ideally, collaborating allows each individual's and team's needs to be satisfied with an "I win, we win" situation. Collaborating on work projects and assignments usually results in resolutions and conclusions that are conflict free.

Group Purpose

All groups share common interests and goals and the members share interactions and interdependence. Groups tend to have a collective identity and a defined structure that defines roles, responsibility and authority.

The conflict-free group working on projects and assignments may not really exist. Company teams do not need to exist without a task. These work tasks can be defined as an activity in which a decision or solution cannot be made without the input of all team members (Fisher, 1971). In some cases, the team project is objective or factual, and in other cases, the task is subjective. To facilitate the accomplishment of a team or department task, group members should do the following (Shaw, 1981):

1. Determine the severity of the task. Will it be easy to accomplish, difficult to accomplish, or extremely complex?
2. Identify the number of alternatives that exist for accomplishing the task.
3. Establish what is important, appealing, interesting or fascinating about the task.
4. Recognize the degree of familiarity team members have with the task.
5. Pinpoint the degree to which the outcome or resolution of the task is found to be acceptable.
6. Verify the amount of authority the team has for executing the task.
7. Take into consideration the degree of ego involvement invested in the task.

The ability to address these seven characteristics allows a team to communicate more efficiently and provides members an opportunity to identify any obstacles or conflicts before they arise and muddle the team into problems, inactivity or failure.

Developing an understanding of the issues within a task or project can lead to the creation of parameters that focus the team on (1) developing skills needed to conduct research about the issue; (2) mapping out work divisions that move the team through identifiable steps toward gathering complete and accurate information; (3) developing role clarifications; and (4) seeking out appropriate, adequate and unambiguous alternatives to reaching successful solutions.

Types of Collaborative Groups

Working groups within an organization can be classified in many ways. When an organization delegates a work project to a group it must consider how much internal specialization and interdependence they require, how much integration and coordination with other parts of the company are needed, and how much power they are allocated (Sundstrom, DeMeuse and Futrell, 1990). Three options for organizing people into work groups are a traditional work group, a traditional team, or a self-managing team. These three groups are part of many company hierarchical systems (McGrath, 1984).

Traditional Work Group
- ✓ *Power in this group is management controlled.*
- ✓ *The leadership is supervisor controlled.*
- ✓ *Decision-making is authoritarian or consultative.*
- ✓ *Activities are independent.*

Traditional Team
- ✓ *Power is linked to organization with some shifted to the team.*
- ✓ *The leadership, with limited power, is selected by the organization.*
- ✓ *Decision-making is consultative or accomplished by consensus.*
- ✓ *Activities are interdependent.*

Self-Managing Team
- ✓ *Power linked to organization, but team has some power and independence.*
- ✓ *Leader is selected by the team.*
- ✓ *Decision-making is democratic or by consensus.*
- ✓ *Activities or tasks are interdependent and coordinated by team members.*

Successful Groups

There are many approaches to formulate defining characteristics of successful groups. In addition to the goal of solidifying solid relationships among group members, Hackman (1987) details five factors necessary for the development of successful groups:

- clear direction and goals;
- good leadership;
- tasks suited for teamwork;
- necessary resources to perform tasks; and
- supportive organizational environment

In "Teamwork: What Can Go Right/What Can Go Wrong" authors Larson and LaFasto (1989) list eight characteristics of team excellence that are like the factors mentioned above.

1. Clear, elevating goals.
2. Results-driven structure.
3. Competent team members.
4. Unified commitment.
5. Collaborative climate.
6. Standards of excellence.
7. External support and recognition.
8. Principled leadership.

Successful groups usually set up standards of excellence and performance so members feel they must perform at their highest levels. These standards are clear and have conflict resolution procedures in place to quickly dissipate any disputes and disagreements.

Psychologists Levi and Slem (1995) determined that evaluation and reward, social relations, organizational support, task characteristics and leadership are factors related to team success. Management must support teams and team leaders must facilitate worker interactions.

Successful teams are the lifeblood of most organizations. Team functioning and behavior have a direct impact on everything from sales and advertising to customer service, to operational costs and profit margins. High-performance teams require unambiguous behaviors and attitudes that might not come naturally to a lot of people. Unfortunately, despite the important role that teams play in organizations, the value of team development is often undervalued.

For individuals to come together as high-performing teams, there must be a culture of trust, respect, and accountability. Each person should be willing to invest in the team in the following ways:

- Use his or her energy, talents, and efforts to achieve the team's goals;
- fulfill his or her individual roles and responsibilities;
- use defined processes and mechanisms that enable the team to function at peak performance.
- expect conflict and deal with it as a positive sign of growth; and
- support each other, follow through on commitments, and take ownership of the team's success.

The value—evident in the results—of this level of team performance to the business can't be understated. That is why it is so important for an organization to provide development opportunities for intact and new teams. Any team development initiative should target three primary characteristics of teamwork that, when combined, can make a team unstoppable.

Collaborating and Not Competing

Many workforce members feel that the way toward advancement is to compete. Many believe that a competitive "race" needs to be won if salary and bonuses are to be gained. Little thought might be given to working together, to create and nurture a work climate of openness and mutual respect. There may be times when employees attempt to use cooperative tactics, plans and strategies, only to be rebuked by competitive individuals.

Differentiating between what employees should share and what they need to keep to themselves constitutes a real business dilemma. Companies often encourage their workforce to place a high value on the positive impact of collaborative action while at the same time allowing them to compete against one another, thereby enhancing their natural motivation to build up their self-esteem.

The purpose of an organization is to prompt large numbers of managers and employees, with diversified experiences and of different standing, to work together to produce competitive products and/or provide exceptional services. Nevertheless, companies have realized over time that some degree of internal competition is helpful. This motivates employees to outperform their colleagues and thus satisfy their individual self-esteem (Nosseir, 2016).

Competition is at the core of a firm's success or failure. Competition determines the appropriateness of a firm's activities that can contribute to its performance, such as innovations, a cohesive culture, or good implementation (Porter, 1985). It seemed to make sense that if companies optimized their revenues streams and developed competitive components they would realize maximum profits and increased margins. However, the incentive to move from the competitive mode to the collaborative mode may more fully represent today's successful business enterprises. Building and managing organizations that broaden connections internally and externally seem to be the norm now.

Many companies, like LEGO and Nike, are finding the best way to design products is in partnership with customers. This has been labeled as co-creation. Co-creation is a management initiative, or form of economic strategy, that brings different parties together to jointly produce a mutually valued outcome (Prahalad and Ramaswamy, 2004). Co-creation blends ideas from direct customers or viewers (who are not the direct users of the product) which in turn creates new ideas for the organization.

As recently as a decade ago, the idea of collaboration meant employees did what the supervisor told them to do. As work culture has evolved, today's organization leaders continue to discover the importance of collaboration as part of the new culture. The heightened productivity levels achieved through joining forces and expanding abilities is key to creating a competitive edge. Here are several ways to gain that edge:

- Rely on subject matter experts and specialists to lead collaborative teams.
- Focus on the long-range view and the incremental steps needed to get there.
- Discover what is working in the company and make it better.
- Share information and successes within the different company departments.
- Be open to customer and client feedback and welcome all support.

To stimulate thinking and discussion about team development and collaboration and competition, the following questions can be presented to a team as part of a professional development (PD) activity:

1. What are you doing best right now on the team?
2. What are you doing to accomplish your load?
3. What factors get in your way to prevent you from working well on the team?
4. How many different tasks are you charged with?
5. How do you desire to receive feedback from other group members?
6. How do you behave when deadlines approach?
7. To whom are you closest on your work team?
8. With whom would you prefer to form a better working relationship?
9. How can you be better with more efficiency?
10. What personal growth efforts are you making on the team and in the organization?

Professional development activities are important because they ensure continual renewal of competence in the profession and should be an ongoing process throughout one's career. The ten PD group discussion questions above can be directed to specific individuals in the group or to the group as a whole. Any member of the team may decline to answer any question, and the format of this PD exercise should aim at making certain that effective understanding takes place.

Functional and Dysfunctional Team Collaborations

Building trust and resolving conflict are two of the most challenging aspects of creating and supporting team collaborations. When professional development activities are presented to organizational teams, criteria must be established to evaluate their effectiveness. William Dryer (1995) has explored the nature of team building and its role in organizations. He has emphasized the needs of the organization and the differing personalities and backgrounds of the workforce. Effective team criteria include (1) clear goals and values understood by the team members; (2) open communication to lead to a climate of support and trust; (3) full participation in decisions and commitments to implement the decisions; and (4) constructive handling of differences.

Symptoms of dysfunctional teams include (1) a loss of production with an increase of complaints; (2) hostility or conflict among members with confusion about tasks and relationships; (3) lack of interest, innovation and effective problem-solving, and, in some cases, apathy; (4) dysfunctional meetings with a high dependency on a team leader, and (5) lack of assuming accountability and losing sight of team goals.

There are many circumstances that create conditions that affect a team's effectiveness and success. Teams can be a powerful vehicle to produce results and build morale. When managed effectively, they can outperform and do more to release creativity and build skills than individuals working alone.

The four most common reasons teams fail are (1) an inability to deal with conflict, (2) ineffective problem-solving skills, (3) a lack of focus on creativity and distinction, and (4) a lack of effective leadership. In addition, psychologist Daniel Goleman (1995) states that developing emotional intelligence can help a person become more self-aware, control emotions and feelings that might contribute to a toxic team environment and be motivated to accept challenging projects while displaying empathy for other team members.

Solid workplace collaborations are built upon a foundation of mutual respect for the differences from all members. Dysfunctional or toxic workplace environments are usually filled with conflict and negativity. Employee dissatisfaction will carry over into the other parts of one's overall well-being. How can team collaborations become functional? Think about these.

> *What is really going on?* Seek out dysfunctional patterns in the team's group dynamics. Where does the team lack direction and what steers them in the wrong direction?
> *What can be changed?* What can be fixed, not fixed, revisited, or resurrected?
> *What can be gleaned from the dysfunction?* How much control does the team have over actions? What can be learned from conflict, roadblocks and obstacles?

Poor Collaboration

Smart organizations bring people together to work smarter. Collaboration drives innovation, better decision making, reduced product cycles, faster to-market success. Delivering collaboration is not always as simple as knowing you need it. Collaboration is certainly a top priority for many business leaders; however, knowing what makes organizations successful can be problematic and complex. Not all companies are alike, and their strategies and technologies can be different. Initiatives involving collaborative efforts can emanate from different departments with different budgets. Distinctive user case scenarios often require different organizational approaches.

1. *Too many cooks*: With collaborative groups, you can end up with too many people trying to lead the team, and not enough members that are willing to take a backseat and do what it takes to get the job done.
2. *Ill will*: Tension from above can flow into other areas of the work environment, causing stress among the rest of the staff, including those that may not even be involved in the collaborative effort.
3. *Not my style*: With collaborate projects there may be a conflict in the working styles of the individuals within the group. This can hold up progress on accomplishing the job at hand, while team members instead get tangled up in conflicts caused by the different ways team members approach the work.
4. *Meeting mania*: Collaboration in the workplace can result in scheduling many meetings; however, some of the most successful enterprises in the world have fewer meetings. The priority is to limit redundancy and foot-dragging. Too many meetings will cloud objectives and expectations.
5. *The road not taken*: When working with others to reach decisions, individuals can become too confident in the accuracy of collective thinking and may choose between the quality of the team work and the quality of workplace relationships and tend to follow majority views without postulating their own ideas.
6. *This is not consensus*: The idea that everyone must sign off on everything is not collaboration, it's officialdom. Honest collaboration is the process of soliciting input and feedback from people who possess different points of view or expertise that can strengthen the work.
7. *Conflict abounds*: People don't always get along and sometimes personalities just don't mesh. Collaborative leaders need to identify situations where team members are in conflict and then develop an action plan that can help everyone to perform optimally.

8. *Inclusion illusion*: This pitfall occurs when a leader embraces the idea of including others in the decision-making process yet does not really want others to participate. Many times, individuals spot this immediately. This precludes non-inclusion, when people are never asked for any input or opinion.

Ineffective collaboration diverts a work team's energy for prolonged periods of time, making it difficult to get tasks accomplished. If individual differences are deepened, morale is destroyed, and team spirit will be undermined. The suppression of open, authentic and honest communication will discourage creativity, innovation and any type of breakthrough thinking. At the worst, poor team collaboration will cause employees to avoid engaging in problem-solving.

The smart organization will train leaders, managers, supervisors and conflict resolvers to ask the following questions:

- What is the work team's greatest strength in working through conflict?
- What is the work team's greatest weakness in working through conflict?
- What types of issues trigger work team conflict?
- What happens in the work team when conflict or poor collaboration first arises?
- Who in the work team gets involved to work on resolution? Who does not, and why?

A horrific example of poor collaboration can be seen with the problems with drinking water in Flint, Michigan. The Flint water crisis started in 2014 when the drinking water source for the city was changed from Lake Huron and the Detroit River to the cheaper Flint River. Because of insufficient water treatment, lead leached from the lead water pipes into the drinking water, affecting over 100,000 residents. Flint has been known for years as a broken industrial city, and its citizens were the victims of what happens when various governmental entities simply can't work with each other. After scientific studies proved lead contamination was present in the water supply, a federal state of emergency was declared in January 2016 and Flint residents were instructed to use only bottled or filtered water for drinking, cooking, cleaning, and bathing, and as early as 2017, the water quality had returned to acceptable levels.

The Flint water crisis highlighted the need for improved risk communication strategies and environmental health infrastructure. As a result of the sustained community involvement and intense media attention, the Water Infrastructure Improvements for the Nation Act of 2016 was passed. A Michigan task force found that this legislation did not provide outcomes because elected officials, Flint's Department of Environmental Protection and community leaders lacked the ability to work together as a collaborative team.

Positive Collaborative Efforts

Organizations have historically recognized that by working together a lot can be accomplished. On the corporate level some of the workforce hurry about chasing their own objectives with only minor concern for the corporate mission. When team members offer distinctive contributions toward a collaborative goal, they share together in the outcome. Several of the benefits of team collaboration are as follows.

Synergy

The essence of synergy is to value differences, to respect them, to build on strengths, to compensate for weaknesses (Covey, 2003). When the whole is greater than the sum of the parts, everyone wins. With collaboration organizations can witness reduced costs, increased capabilities, and more flexibility to adapt to changing requirements.

Distribution

One of the greatest benefits of collaboration is that everyone gets a piece of the work pie. The project at hand isn't solely resting on the shoulders of one individual. This can result in enhanced individual productivity.

Innovation

Team collaboration offers multiple perspectives for innovation and problem solving. By leveraging these perspectives to validate ideas and propose solutions, problem solving is taken to the highest level. Another aspect of innovation is that the workforce feels valued and respected for their ideas and input.

Competition

Creating effective collaborative structures can increase competition among teams, departments and divisions to come up with great ideas, products, services and strategies to address company issues. This need not be viewed negatively. The increased competition among work groups can generate data that solves problems with amazing accomplishments.

Acceleration

With a collaborative culture the ability to bring products and services to the market faster is a big plus. Teamwork and communication will speed up the entire process and make it easier to achieve organizational success. The company's ability to create value accelerates as a result.

Positive collaboration is not micromanagement. Some organizations think that collaboration means that every word or change requires a sign-off before anything gets done. Successful efforts for true collaboration require leadership that is always looking to create stellar opportunities to engage the workforce and to eliminate barriers. Organizational culture that encourages employee involvement and participation is a necessary support for good teamwork. These supportive organizations employ managers who are less likely to resist using teams and are open to the creation of self-managing teams.

Collaborating to Get More

Collaborating to achieve more requires cohesion. Workforce team members should have defined individual roles and a clear understanding of their position. To get the most out of collaboration each team must have a designated leader(s) who will lead from the front. This will prevent sabotage by unnecessary turf battles with the group. To achieve wins and successes, team leaders will need to ease up on control and embrace the collective wisdom of all members without attempting to wield authority. This may sound like a different type of organizational thinking or strategy; however, these types of new approaches can result in significant gains when the following are addressed (Diamond, 2010).

1. Focus on goals.
2. Every project or situation is different.
3. Work incrementally.
4. Find standards.
5. Be transparent and constructive, not manipulative.
6. Always communicate, state the obvious and frame the vision.
7. Embrace differences.

Cohesive team members work with their strengths rather than working around their weaknesses.

When people on teams are connected through their potencies, each one is set up for success because they work on tasks that play to those respective strengths.

....

The Space Creature (Michalko, 2006)

Have a group imagine a creature living on another planet with a different atmosphere in a distant solar system. Draw a picture of the creature you imagine. Then share your drawing with the group. You may discover that most people drew creatures that resemble life as we understand it, even though we are free to think up anything. Rather than creating something that is idiosyncratic and unpredictable, most people create creatures that have a great deal in common with one another and the properties of typical Earth animals. People drawing space creatures could have tapped into any existing knowledge base to get an idea for the general shape of their creature, and each person could access something different and novel. But most people do not, and so they wind up drawing creatures that have similar properties to creatures on Earth.

....

The above group exercise exhibits a phenomenon called *structured imagination*. Structured imagination refers to the fact that even when we use our imagination to develop new ideas, those ideas are heavily structured in highly predictable ways according to existing concepts, categories and stereotypes. It is likely that the drawings might be totally different if they were first discussed in a collaborative group and then designed with individual input from each member.

A structured approach in collaboration involves many rules, guidelines, and restrictions. An unstructured approach usually has some guidelines and best practices, but usually leaves the workforce unregulated in terms of how they can collaborate and use internal tools and platforms.

Collaboration and Achievement

Many companies are looking for robust ways to foster collaborative teams to undertake their tasks and projects. There are many studies that demonstrate the benefits of collaboration and connectedness among a group of people. Success depends on which part of the problem-solving process people are engaged in and the search for information or using the information to come up with solutions. Diversity among team members can assist or hamper achievement. Dr. Jay Hall (2009) found direct connections between achievement and the ability to connect with people. To be effective in collaborative groups means to take advantage of connecting with people with varying aspirations and styles. The practical skills of connection involve finding common ground, keeping communication simple, being authentic and providing inspiration.

Many companies exist to assist organizations in developing great collaborations; an example is Phi-Services, LLC, a unique company based in New York City that connects people with technology. It brings a wealth of experience to an exclusive focus on the world of collaboration through the effective implementation, integration and adoption of collaborative, interactive technologies. As a collaborative group, this organization considers strong, on-going relationships an important measure of success. Working closely with companies, it endeavors to develop a strategy that starts with an understanding of how the company works today, builds on what needs to be done and leads to change. This and other technologies assist with employee collaboration and can preclude possibilities for the development of conflict.

Virtual Teams

The availability of communication technology has led to the creation of virtual teams. Virtual teams are any teams whose member interactions are mediated by time, distance and technology. Such teams can save organizations the challenges and cost of setting up additional infrastructure in locations where they want a presence, but a physical space is not needed. Technology and accessibility to global talent have made it possible to make this a sustainable phenomenon of having many employees, and it is turning out to be the optimal way "remote working" can be used by having a dedicated resource pool. As businesses are hosting most of their infrastructure online people across the world can simultaneously access the same project and chat as easily as if they were in the same room together. Digital workplaces and virtual teams are now popular options for forward-thinking companies. Typical types of virtual team meetings that are created by virtual information technology are outlined by Mittleman and Briggs (1999).

Type of Meeting	Example
STSP—Same time, same place	Face-to-face meeting
STDP—Same time, different place	Videoconferencing
DTSP—Different time, same place	Computer databases
DTDP—Different time, different place	Intranet bulletin board

The challenges of virtual teams are both common and manageable.

Communication styles may be different: Everyone has different preferences when it comes to communication. Virtual team employees must understand what the expected level of communication is. Leading a virtual team requires a strong manager to pull things together and create a productive team. Virtual teams usually lack the informal, everyday conversations that co-located employees take for granted. They may be deprived of nonverbal cues that indicate whether a colleague is on board or annoyed.

Deindividuation: Working within the virtual team structure may result in the loss of self-awareness and evaluation apprehension caused by employees feeling anonymous. One of the impacts of deindividuation is that employees may be more willing to say things they would not say in face-to-face interactions and that could precipitate a rise in a host of negative emotions and eventually in conflict scenarios.

Distracting technology environments: Virtual teams often struggle with distracting environments. Each distraction diminishes the efficiency of usually well-performing employees.

Lack of trust: Individuals can't see what others are doing, and responses may not be immediate. Trust can be a problem when only some team members are virtual. Awareness of each other's contributions helps to build trust. As well as setting clear goals and expectations, leaders should make sure that individual roles and responsibilities are publicized within the team.

Missing an office culture: It is difficult to create an effective office culture when there is no office. Colleagues may go days without "speaking" to each other and it's likely that they'll never meet in person.

Loss of team spirit: Cohesiveness builds gradually in face-to-face teams, while virtual teams often feel like no more than globally dispersed individuals working on the same project. Virtual leaders are responsible for creating a clear and compelling direction for the team and making sure each individual is connected to the team vision. Team members' individual goals should be linked to the team's overall goal and to each other.

Meeting schedules: Since many virtual teams find themselves working from different places in the world, setting up meetings can be difficult. When teams work on different schedules, everyone must compromise.

Six Thinking Hats

Thinking is the ultimate human resource, yet the main difficulty of thinking is confusion. This is especially true in collaborative group work. When we attempt to do too much at once, information, emotion, logic and creativity all battle for space and priority. Often, the best decisions come from changing the way that we think about problems and examining them from different viewpoints.

Six Thinking Hats can help to look at problems from different perspectives, but one at a time, to avoid confusion from too many angles crowding your thinking. It's also a powerful decision-checking technique in group situations, as everyone explores the situation from each perspective at the same time. Six Thinking Hats was created by Edward de Bono (1985) as a problem-solving approach to more creatively manage conflicts. It empowers us to move outside our habitual thinking style and to look at things from several different perspectives. Teams often reach a successful solution or outcome from a rational, positive viewpoint, but it can also pay to consider a problem from other angles. Each hat represents a different perspective. Each team member wears each hat in turn.

Here's a brief description of the Six Thinking Hats.

- **The White Hat**
The White Hat calls for information known or needed. Offers objective facts and figures and can be used near the beginning of a meeting to establish relevant data.

- **The Red Hat**
The Red Hat signifies feelings, hunches, instincts and intuition. The emotions are used to get people's reactions to ideas.

- **The Black Hat**
The Black Hat is judgment, the devil's advocate or why something may not work. Used when critical viewpoints or ideas are needed to decrease the chances of making poor decisions.

- **The Yellow Hat**

The Yellow Hat symbolizes brightness and optimism. Used to help identify the values of ideas and plans. Helps to counterbalance the judgmental thinking of the Black Hat.

- **The Green Hat**

The Green Hat focuses on creativity: the possibilities, alternatives and new ideas. Used to generate and produce fresh ideas and new directions.

- **The Blue Hat**

The Blue Hat is used to manage the thinking process. Sets objectives, outlines the issues, summarizes and draws conclusions at the end.

By having collaborative group members wearing and changing these hats, the work team will benefit by maximizing productive collaboration and minimizing counterproductive interactions and behaviors. Conflict issues, problems, decisions and opportunities are worked on systematically using parallel thinking as a group or team tends to generate more and better ideas and solutions. Work meetings can be much shorter and more productive and stimulate innovation by generating many ideas. This type of collaborative and lateral thinking can assist with (1) spotting opportunities where others see only problems; (2) thinking clearly and objectively; (3) viewing problems from new and unusual angles; (4) making thorough evaluations; and (5) achieving significant and meaningful results in a shorter period of time.

One of the major purposes of the Six Thinking Hats is the utilization of parallel thinking. Parallel thinking can be viewed as a thinking process where focus is split in specific directions. When done in a group it effectively avoids the consequences of the adversarial and divisive approach. In adversarial debate, the objective is to prove or disprove statements put forward by disputants. With parallel thinking, practitioners put forward as many statements as possible in several (preferably more than two) parallel tracks. This leads to greater exploration of a subject where all participants can contribute, in parallel, with knowledge, facts, and feelings.

Using parallel thinking and the Six Thinking Hats, individuals in groups can change their thinking. If a member of a group has been persistently negative, de Bono suggests that the person be asked to take off the Black Thinking Hat. This is a signal to the person that he or she is being negative. The person may be also asked to put on the Yellow Thinking Hat. That would be a direct request to be positive. It is in this way the six hats provide an idiom that is definite without being offensive. What is most important is that the idiom doesn't threaten a person's ego or personality. As role-play, the concept of the hats makes it possible to request certain types of thinking.

Things do go wrong at work. Hopefully, executives, managers, workers, teams, departments and divisions have a structure in place to deal with problems. How organizations deal with problems sets the tone for how the entire workforce behaves. Dealing effectively with problems in collaboration with each other will improve morale and promote accountability and calculated risk-taking.

Dr. de Bono's Six Thinking Hats is a powerful technique for looking at decision making from different points of view for it allows emotion and skepticism to be brought into what might normally be a purely rational process, and it opens up the opportunity for creativity within decision making.

Decisions made using the Six Thinking Hats technique can be sounder and more resilient than would otherwise be the case. The technique can also help avoid possible pitfalls before commitments to a decision are made.

The Fieldtown Baseball Field

The community directors of Fieldtown are considering whether they should build a new baseball park. The economy of the town is not doing well since the local technology company left and took 2,500 jobs with them. An extremely large lot in the town is ripe for development. As part of their decision-making process, the community directors adopt the Six Thinking Hats technique.

Wearing the **White Hat**, they investigate the data that they have. They can see that the available space in the town is unused, and they compute that by the time the new stadium would be completed, jobs and revenues would increase. They also note that the economic outlook would include new parking ventures, concession stands, janitorial services, and security. Steady growth is predicted.

Thinking with the **Red Hat**, some of the directors state that the proposed stadium plans look dreadful and dark. They worry that prospective fans would find it a lackluster venue.

When they think with the **Black Hat**, they wonder whether the timing of the building of this stadium could be wrong. The town's economy may spiral downward, in which case the stadium would not sustain a fan base and sit empty for a long time. If the stadium is unattractive that would be another reason the fans might stay home.

Wearing the positive **Yellow Hat**, however, the directors of the town know that other towns that have embarked on a similar venture are making healthy profits and bringing jobs back. If the stadium is well-built, attractive and includes the latest retractable roof, it could attract some good baseball teams.

With **Green Hat** thinking, they consider whether they should redesign the stadium to cater to companies by offering luxury boxes and other amenities to make it more appealing. They could also construct new prestige office space that would appeal to new clients.

The executive director of the community panel of the meeting wears the **Blue Hat** to keep the discussion moving and ideas flowing, encouraging the others to switch their thinking between the different perspectives.

Having examined their options from numerous viewpoints, the community directors have a much more detailed picture of possible outcomes and can make their decision accordingly.

• •

6

Conflict Resolution Approaches

Strategies, Purposes, Practices

There has been much research and publication on the value of conflict resolution, the strategies, purposes and practitioners. The value of conflict resolution cannot be extolled and celebrated enough. Every organization has a strategy for managing conflict. Three strategies are by power contests, by rights contests and by reconciling interests. "Unmanaged conflict is the largest reducible cost in organizations today, and the least recognized" (Dana, 2001).

- Dominating organization: one in which power contests are the prevailing approach to resolving conflicts.
- Litigating organization: one in which rights contests are the prevailing approach to resolving conflicts.
- Mediating organization: one in which interest reconciliation is the prevailing approach to resolving conflict.

Many organizations tend to rely on professional conflict management specialists that work within structured and formal channels. Some HR departments hire these specialists to handle conflict issues. Other organizations rely on department, division, or team managers who can effectively manage the everyday conflicts. Some believe they are better equipped to work on conflict issues because they know the disputant parties and, possibly, the nature and issues of the dispute.

The Mediation Training Institute in St. Petersburg, Florida (Dana, 2001), indicates the three dimensions in every organization in which its conflict management strategy is imbedded are competencies, structure and culture dimensions. Competence refers to the employees' ability to manage conflict. Structure refers to the formal design of the organizational system. Culture refers to the norms and shared values and attitudes that influence workplace conflict behaviors.

Conflict resolution recognizes that conflict is a normal and natural phenomenon and when it is handled effectively can create opportunities for resolution, growth and new and continual learning. The five basic values underlying conflict resolution are as follows (Deutsch and Coleman, 2000).

Reciprocity	Each party in a dispute agrees to treat the other with the same fairness that they would normally expect.
Human Equality	Each person is equally entitled to be treated justly, with respect, with consideration for their needs and entitled to such liberties as freedom of conscience, thought and expression.
Shared Community	There is mutual recognition of being a part of a broader community that members wish to preserve.
Fallibility	Reasonable people will understand that their own judgment as well as the judgment of others may be fallible.
Non-Violence	Coercive tactics will not be employed by any party in a dispute to obtain agreement or consent.

Organizational conflicts can arise in a host of ways. Unsatisfactory contracts will result in damaging relationships between buyers, sellers, vendors and agencies. Disagreements can occur between subdivisions as they relate to scope of territory, resources or funding. Employee conflicts can develop over salary compensation, allocation of benefits, and work load. In some companies there may be conflicts between labor and management. Negotiation and mediation specialists in organizations can resolve a broad set of conflict issues. The rationalist tradition has dominated the study of conflict resolution in organizations since Frederick Taylor (1912 [1984]) laid the foundations for instrumental-rational organization theory. From this perspective, conflict threatens efficiency and conflict resolution comprises specialized tools necessary to control conflict or channel conflict into productive pursuits.

Organizations are living systems consisting of interacting units performing a task in a mutually dependent manner within a structure of scarce resources (Katz and Kahn, 1957) and it seems commonplace to suggest that conflicts would be present in such a setting. Once the parties in the company are in a situation of goal incompatibility, their conflict can develop in a dynamic fashion, initiating valuable and much-needed constructive changes or leading to escalating strategies and destructive consequences (Deutsch, 1969).

The Flowchart of Conflict

Conflict Origins

Limited Resources	Unmet Needs	Different Values
Time	Empathy	Principles
Budget	Power/Control	Work Ethics
Personnel	Comradery	Beliefs

Conflict Occurs

Soft Responses	Hard Responses	Disciplined Responses
Withdrawal	Aggression	Compromise
Denial	Threats/Bullying	Understanding
Evasion	Anger	Resolution

In a complex work environment, tasks are accomplished through the collaborative efforts of many. Differences are a positive force if one knows how to harness them. Among the three types of responses in the diagram above, the disciplined responses are the desirable ones, and these are dependent upon one's ability to develop good interpersonal work relationships and create rapport in team or project work. Developing self-awareness, analyzing conflict situations, and consciously selecting and using productive communication strategies are strengths that will be useful in all task-related assignments.

Conflict Resolution Techniques

The living systems in organizations will eventually see disagreements and conflicts. Conflict and disagreement are not only inevitable, but fundamental to successful company change. Since any working group of people possesses multiple realities, any collective change attempt will necessarily involve conflict (Fullan, 1991). When conflicts are not addressed in the workplace, they will escalate and contaminate the work environment. As time goes on, tensions build and the conflict becomes worse. Here are some simple tips to address conflicts:

- Set up a time and place to talk for an extended span without outside interruptions.
- Listen carefully to give your complete attention to the person who is talking.
- Clarify what the disagreement is.
- Establish a common goal for both parties.
- Provide guidance, if you're in a leadership position.
- Discuss ways to meet common goals and determine the barriers to the common goal.
- Agree on the best way to resolve the conflict.
- Address sensitive issues in private.
- Reach out to a third party if no resolution can be agreed to.
- Celebrate resolution.

Getting together to work on conflicts in an organization is the recognition that when agreements are reached the workplace can run smoothly. Conflict resolution is not confrontational or win-lose. It does not mean getting your way, no matter what, or walking away with less, if there is more to gain. It is not a triumph of the powerful over the weak or a battle or an intimidation.

One of the largest problems in the implementation of a conflict resolution program involves increased organizational complexity. Extensive changes and reforms in the organization can cause confusion about the lines of authority and accountability. Many additional problems can arise when the company embarks upon a new course of improvement and/or when there are personnel changes at the top of the company.

Negotiation

Negotiation is the ability to settle a dispute with another person without engaging a mediator, attorney or arbitrator. Recently, I brought in four shirts to my dry cleaner, and when I picked them up, took them home, and removed the plastic, I discovered that one of my favorite shirts, which I have had dry-cleaned before, had shrunk. I returned with my shirt to the store and informed them of the problem. They denied that they were responsible and said that I must have brought the shirt in that way. Our conversation became heated and neither of us got anywhere until I mentioned that I would no longer be a customer and I would file a complaint with the consumer affairs division that licenses this enterprise. The owner then asked me what I wanted. I mentioned that the shirt cost $49 and I wanted that in repayment. The response was that the shirt was no longer new, and the store offered me $20. We continued to talk and we eventually agreed on $35 for the shrunken garment and a $15 voucher for my next dry-cleaning bill. Our verbal exchange to reach a win-win agreement is called negotiation.

Negotiation is a communication interaction that involves individuals that have conflicting goals or interests and the object is to reach an agreement. An important part of negotiating is to understand what is and what is not negotiable. A former *Washington Post* editor, Robert Estabrook, once said, "He who has learned to disagree without being disagreeable has discovered the most valuable secret of a diplomat." *Integrative* or collaborative negotiation is an interest-based strategy that allows for the "pie" to be enlarged through communication and usually results in win-win settlements. Dividing the fixed "pie" is *distributive* negotiation and usually ends up in a win-lose settlement. Some researchers believe that people will not negotiate with you unless they believe you can help them or hurt them. In his book *You Can Negotiate Anything*, author Herb Cohen (1980) states that anything that was negotiated is negotiated. In most organizations the following are negotiable.

- Price
- Terms
- Delivery
- Quality
- Service
- Training
- Resources
- Scope of Involvement

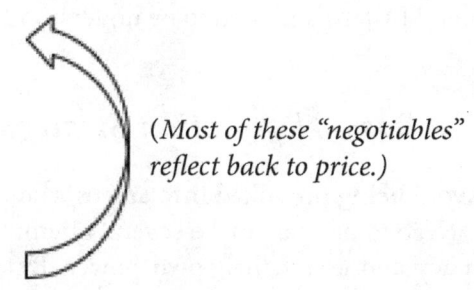

(*Most of these "negotiables" reflect back to price.*)

Members of a workforce that face conflict can use integrative negotiation techniques to reach satisfactory agreements and resolutions. These are internal negotiations and can be worked out in a neutral place in the organization like a small conference or meeting room. These types of negotiations provide the parties time to explore their mutual interests in achieving win-win closure, so they can return to work with realized mutual gains. The major benefit of integrative negotiation is that it combines formal bargaining techniques with basic and concrete interpersonal communication skills. The parties explore their interests to see what is compatible or incompatible and can discuss and explore many possible options that will satisfy their interests. This clear communication can preserve and improve the relationship between the individuals and that, in turn, is a huge benefit to the organization.

Receive and Then Deliver

The research on negotiation effectiveness repeatedly underscores one simple fact—negotiators focus more than average on receiving as opposed to delivering information (Shell, 2006). The questions asked have an important purpose; they are usually designed to elicit real information ("When can you make delivery?" or "How did you come up with that number?"). The next step is to test their understanding of what the other side has said. Posting questions and receiving clarification regarding others' answers have obvious benefits in the terms of data flow. However, these techniques also give negotiators additional time to plan and execute their next moves.

Information exchange is vital to highlight and define people's interest and issues. This back-and-forth flow of information is a strategic and slow process and often relies on all parties trusting each other. Seek first to understand (listen) and then to be understood (communicate).

Three Basic Negotiation Strategies

1. **Avoid being provoked into an emotional response.**

    Negotiators may make several attempts to question each other's legitimacy and assert their own power. By challenging, demeaning, and criticizing tactics, the other party (whether consciously or not) may be attempting to provoke you into an emotional response that will shift the balance of power in their favor.

    How can you respond?

    ✓ Interrupt the tactic by taking a break, which should give everyone time to gain control of their emotions, in addition to halting any momentum that is going against you.

✓ Call them out for this ploy!
✓ Sidestep the tactic by shifting the focus back to the issue at hand.

2. Stick to value-creating strategies.
Negotiators who understand the importance of collaborating with one another to create value might often abandon that approach during dispute resolution. These negotiators tend to look at the dispute resolution process as a win-lose battle. You should endeavor to find the same set of value-creation opportunities in disputes as you do in deals. Disputants may also be able to create value by trading on their differing preferences and priorities.

3. Employ time to your advantage.
What negotiators may think about the dispute resolution process may change over time because of our experiences in dealing with the conflict and with the other party. Negotiations take time, and if there is no progress in the bargaining, work slowly to work through differences because new, creative proposals may crop up over time.

Competitive and Cooperative Negotiation

Negotiation is a psychological investigation and preparation is the key to success. When the pressure builds, one does not rise to the occasion, one falls to the highest level of preparation (Voss, 2016). Competitive negotiation usually involves tangible issues and assets. In many companies these tangibles involve material things such as money, time, space, workload, and other resource-based things. These are important conflicts and as they occur they have the potential to affect the individuals' relationships. Competitive negotiators believe they must not show weakness in their positions or offer concessions too soon (Wall, 1985). These types of negotiations tend to be win-lose, as they often proceed from a "fixed-pie outlook."

Cooperative negotiation is a collaborative form and works best when the employees and managers trust each other and where mutually satisfactory agreements are possible. The disputants in these types of negotiations assume that win-win solutions are always possible, and they work to achieve them. However, a bad or unproductive negotiation can damage a working relationship for a long time. Each of us occasionally engages in an exchange with someone over an issue in a way that makes future problem-solving difficult (Fisher & Brown, 1988). To avoid sacrificing a relationship for any short-term gain, one should use negotiating techniques that protect one's interests, and, at the same time, are consistent with building good working relationships.

A True Negotiation Situation?

Here are three hypothetical situations. Decide which describe the beginnings of a true negotiation (Ré, 2003).

- ✓ A little girl goes with her dad to a shopping center, and she asks, "Hey, Daddy, can I have an ice-cream cone?" He replies, "You want one now?" "Yes!" she urges him. "I won't tell Mom."
- ✓ A man's boss calls him into the office and out of the blue says, "Joe, I'd like to offer you a raise." "You want to offer me a raise?" he asks skeptically.
- ✓ A prisoner in jail calls out to his jailer, "Hey! Give me a cigarette!" The jailer shakes his head. "You know the rules. No cigarettes." "Aw, come on," says the prisoner.

All three scenarios have the potential to be negotiated. They can be categorized as a request, an offer, and a demand, and both sides, in each situation, have something positive to gain.

The point of negotiation is to finalize an agreement that benefits both parties. Ury and Fisher (2001) in their book contend that having a Best Alternative to a Negotiated Agreement (BATNA) lets individuals feel more comfortable in a negotiation. The more important a negotiation is, the more essential it is to have an alternative that is equally as attractive as a negotiated settlement. In addition to creating a BATNA, other negotiation objectives include the following:

1. The extensive planning of the content of the negotiation.
2. Recognizing the stages of negotiation.
3. Making a business decision before determining the negotiation strategy.
4. Identifying the communication styles of your counterpart.
5. Adjusting your own communication styles to achieving desired results.
6. Exhibiting knowledge of the principles of active listening.
7. Planning a strategy for face-to-face negotiations as well as

those negotiations supplemented using other media (email, teleconferencing, videoconferencing, etc.).
8. Demonstrating an understanding of team negotiation.
9. Recognizing ploys and tactics used by negotiators and knowing how to counter them.
10. Understanding the role culture plays in negotiation.

Factors Affecting the Negotiation Process

Skills of the Negotiators	Planning
Organizational Factors	Legal Factors
The Current Economy	Strategy and Tactics
Cultural and Personal Factors	Place, Time, Other Constraints

Most salespeople, business owners and organizations hear statements like this every day: *"What's your best bottom line price?" "That's too expensive." "Your competitor's selling the same thing for much less."*

Here are three strategies that will help you improve your negotiation skills (Lewicki, B. Barry, and D. Saunders, 2016).

1. **Learn to flinch.**

The flinch is one of the oldest negotiation tactics but one of the least used. A flinch is a visible reaction to an offer or price. The objective of this negotiation tactic is to make the other people feel uncomfortable about the offer they presented. Here is an example of how it works.

A supplier quotes a price for a specific service. Flinching means you respond by exclaiming, *"You want how much?"* You must appear shocked and surprised that they could be bold enough to request that figure.

2. **The person with the most information usually does better.**

You need to learn as much as you can about the other person's situation. This is a particularly important negotiation tactic for salespeople. Ask your prospect more questions about their purchase. Learn what is important to them as well as what they need and want.

3. **Maintain your walk away power.**

It is better to walk away from a negotiation than make too large a concession or give too deep a discount your product or service. Negotiating is a way of life in some cultures. And most people negotiate in some way almost every day. Apply these negotiation strategies and you will notice a difference in your negotiation skills almost immediately.

bring to the team. They should not be chosen based on their position, title, or skills they brought to prior negotiations, if such attributes do not add value to the negotiation in which you're about to enter. Nor should anyone who is too independent be placed on the team. Someone who is too independent could prove to be an issue.

An integrative or collaborative team negotiation begins with the premise that developing and preserving relationships is a key value of the process. Negotiation teams using an integrative model educate each other about their needs and engage in problem-solving to reach a resolution that will integrate their needs. When the negotiators explore their interests, they will find that they share interests and that solutions beyond fixed pie choices are possible (Griffith & Goodwin, 2016).

Since negotiation team solutions can be complicated, it might be prudent to keep the teams relatively small. Identifying the various roles that need to be represented will help to determine which and how many people should be on the team. With a large team, the hardest negotiation is often before you get to the table. Assigning roles on the team is essential.

It may not always be clear when an organization should assemble a negotiation team. According to Cornell University professor Elizabeth Mannix (2004), negotiating as a team can be preferable to going it alone in the following situations:

- complex negotiations that require diverse knowledge;
- negotiations with great potential for creativity and value creation;
- negotiations with multiple constituents who all have a stake in the outcome;
- international contexts in which team negotiations are the norm; and
- negotiations in which there is enough time to coordinate a team approach.

Working as part of a negotiation team has its positives. In negotiation, two or more heads can be better than one. Some researchers have found that teams are better at effective negotiation strategies such as developing tradeoffs among issues as compared to solo negotiators. Teams tend to be better than solo negotiators at exchanging information with counterparts and making accurate judgments, and they tend to reach better outcomes. Teams also tend to feel more powerful, less competitive, and less pressured than individual negotiators. The tendency of teams to outperform solo negotiators has been attributed to several factors, including the high economic goals that teams set for themselves, their heightened sense of competition, and members' tendency to challenge one another's views. It may also be important that those participating in a team negotiation monitor one another's behavior, while individuals often negotiate unobserved by others in their organizations. Monitoring tends to amplify the social norms, or behavioral expectations, that are so important in a negotiation (Thompson, Peterson & Brodt, 1996).

Framing in Negotiation

One of the most important issues in negotiation is framing. A *frame* is the subjective mechanism through which negotiators evaluate and make sense of situations, leading them to pursue or avoid subsequent action. A frame offers perspective by managing the alignment of the observer in relation to an issue. Framing is about focusing, shaping, and organizing the world around us, and because people have different backgrounds, experiences, expectations, and needs, they often frame people, events and processes differently. It directs the observer to focus on a feature of an issue within the frame and to disregard other features of the same issue that fall outside this frame.

Negotiation framing is the process of highlighting what will be discussed during the negotiation, and preemptive framing is the process incurred to better position oneself to frame the negotiation—attempting to frame the points of discussion that you'd like to be addressed prior to the opposing negotiator doing so. Just as a point of reference, preemptive framing can also occur any time prior to a negotiation. Preemptive framing is so important in the negotiation process, and if done right, it can position you and your agenda to be viewed in a more favorable light than what otherwise might have been the case.

How parties frame and define a negotiating issue or problem is a clear reflection of what they define as critical to negotiating objectives, what their expectations and preferences are for certain possible outcomes, what information they seek and use to argue their case, the procedures they use to present their case, and the way they evaluate the outcomes and resolutions achieved (Lewicki, Barry and Saunders, 2007).

Types of Frames
- Substantive: what the negotiation is about.
- Outcome: a party's predisposition to achieving a specific result or outcome.
- Aspiration: a predisposition toward satisfying a broader set of interests or needs.
- Process: how the parties will go about resolving the issues (concern about how the deliberations will proceed and be managed).
- Identity: how the parties define *who they are.*
- Characterization: how the parties define the other side (shaped by information, experience, reputation, perception).
- Loss-gain: how the parties define the risk or reward associated with outcomes.

How Frames Work in Negotiation
- ✓ Negotiators can use more than one frame.
- ✓ Mismatches in frames between parties are sources of conflict.
- ✓ Certain types of frames may lead to particular types of agreements.
- ✓ Specific frames may be likely used with certain types of issues.
- ✓ Parties are likely to assume a particular frame because of various factors.

Making sense of complex realities and defining them in ways that are meaningful in a negotiation is what framing is all about. Some prescriptive advice about problem framing for the negotiator include the below:

- ✓ Frames shape what the parties define as the key issues and how they talk about them.
- ✓ Both parties have frames.
- ✓ Frames are controllable, at least to some degree.
- ✓ Conversations change and transform frames in ways negotiators may not be able to predict but may be able to control.

For example, if a negotiator raises his voice and exhibits heated anger, instead of responding angrily to that tirade, a negotiator can reframe the issue by calmly asking how the other person would choose to improve the situation, thus moving the focus back to the issue at hand. Framing that takes another person's viewpoint into account and offers solutions that give everyone something of value is the best example of a win-win negotiation technique.

Questioning in Negotiation

Since information is the lifeblood of negotiation, asking questions the right way is both an art and a science in providing information to discern problems, concerns and needs. Ask the question the wrong way and your counterpart might become defensive and withdrawn, and you face stalls, objections and needless complications (Bednarz, 2011). The following are smart, effective and useful questions to pose.

Open-ended questions
These are the kinds of questions that require a detailed answer and cannot be simply answered with a *"Yes"* or *"No"* response. They consist of asking who, what, where, when, why, and how. The respondent has no alternative but to provide some detail.
Example: *"How did you arrive at that particular price regarding the stocking fees?"*

Open opportunity questions
This form of question invites the person to participate and offer their views.
Example: *"Help me understand how you came up with that solution."*

Probing deeper questions
Ask these questions when you need to gain a better insight into a person's thought process to further illuminate their rationale or position.
Example: *"Could you provide us with more detail in how you analyzed the data?"*

Sequential questions
Sometimes, it can be very good strategy to ask a series of questions to lead up to and achieve a particular result conclusion. Generally, it might be a good idea to plan these in advance.
Example: *"When will the second shipment be ready to be sent to us?"*

Outcome questions
This type of question is used at the settlement or resolution stage to plan to achieve something.
Example: *"What benefit are you expecting out of this?"*

Alternative questions

Ask these questions when you give your counterpart a choice of two or more alternative answers to obtain specific information on what they want.

Example: *"Is less input or greater productivity more important to you?"*

To obtain information from the other side, it could be helpful to map out several general questions.

- It appears that _____ is very valuable to you.
- I get the feeling you don't like _____.
- It seems that you value _____.
- It seems like _____ makes it easier.
- It appears you are reluctant to _____.

As an example, if one is trying to negotiate the addition of some new financial software to the company accounting division and you know that the assistant director of finance is opposed to this move, the prepared questions may include "It appears that you are reluctant to abandon the current spreadsheet software for this finance suite" or "It appears that the stability of the current software is very valuable to you."

With adequate questioning preparation, negotiators can look beyond the other side's firmly stated positions and explore their underlying motivations.

Listening in Negotiation

Mahatma Gandhi said, "Three-fourths of the miseries and misunderstandings in the world will disappear if we step into the shoes of our adversaries and understand their viewpoint" (Fischer, 1962). When we can listen to others and comprehend the other point of view we often find our own point of view changed.

Excellent listening skills help in improved communication, professional growth, career satisfaction and successful negotiations. Listening is the process of receiving, understanding, remembering, evaluating and responding to verbal (spoken or written) and/or nonverbal messages (DeVito, 2019). Negotiators must recognize that listening is not a passive activity. When conflicts arise in a business and they need to be resolved, active listening will play a vital role in reaching compromise. Active listening serves the major function of being able to check for understanding. The simplest way to check for understanding is to paraphrase the speaker's meaning. Stating in your own words what you think the speaker means assists in understanding and shows interest in the speaker. A good way to start this process is to state, "So what I hear you saying is…"

Effective active listening involves not only tuning into others but tuning into ourselves (Burley-Allen, 1995). Increasing our self-awareness makes us more empathetic people, team workers, and negotiators. Listening within the work context is the main process by which we gain an understanding of the needs, demands, and preferences of the stakeholders through direct interaction.

Active listening is all about building rapport, understanding, and trust, and by utilizing these skills, one will become a better listener and hear what the other person is saying, not just what one thinks the other person is saying.

Examples of Effective Listening
- A negotiator repeats a patron's problem or complaint back to her to reassure her that she has been heard.
- A meeting facilitator encourages a reticent group member to share her views about a proposal.
- An interviewer asks a follow-up question to gain further clarification on the ways in which a candidate has applied a critical skill in the past.
- A supervisor summarizes what her team has said during a staff meeting and asks if she has heard things correctly.
- At a client meeting, a salesperson asks an open-ended question like "What can I do to serve you better?" and encourages his counterpart to express any concerns fully.
- A negotiator pays careful attention to his counterpart and asks clarifying questions on the information he is receiving.
- A negotiator asks for help in understanding why the new price is 12 percent higher and frames it as an open opportunity question.

Examples of Non-Listening Behaviors
- *Pseudo listeners* are those individuals who pretend to listen and accompany this fake listening by nodding their head.
- *Selective listeners* key into what interests them and what they wish to hear. They use invisible ear muffs to close off listening.

- *Monopolizing listeners* talk a great deal and don't give others time to speak. They are ear hogs.
- *Defensive listeners* wait to hear something they can attack and criticize. They cherry-pick what is offered and then zing imaginary darts at the speaker.

Negotiators who engage in active listening practice completely focusing on listening designed to keep their mind from drifting off. Reflective listening shows that the conflict resolver understands what has been said and they can exhibit emotional intelligence by deep thinking about the emotions behind the words. For example, an administrative assistant may be complaining about the boss because he feels unappreciated. Poor listening leads to assumptions and misunderstandings which lead to errors, ineffective decisions, and/or costly mistakes. On an interpersonal level, poor listening leads to hurt feelings and a loss of team cohesion. This deteriorates trust and weakens communication even further.

When negotiators, conflict resolvers, peer review panels, or human resources people use active listening skills to gather information, remember, understand and make decisions, they should be aware that the meaning in the message is not only in the words; it's also in the speaker's nonverbal behavior, and that is why it is always preferable to meet face to face. Listening with empathy and an open mind is difficult. Sometimes it is difficult to listen to the other side when their messages and arguments are viewed as attacking or demeaning yours. Open-minded and fair listening requires the following:

1. Avoiding the filtering out of difficult or undesirable messages: avoid distorting messages through oversimplification and the tendency to eliminate details.
2. Recognizing one's own biases: this can interfere with accurate listening and cause message distortion.
3. Avoiding quick judgments: it is important to delay both positive and negative evaluations until one fully understands the intention and content of the message being transmitted.
4. Avoiding the tendency to reconfigure messages so they fit into your realm of needs and values: this is a tendency to reconstruct that message so it reflects your own attitudes and prejudices.

Negotiation requires hard and focused listening, the simplest way to discern needs and discover facts. In conflict situations, even those involving a company mediator or third-party negotiation facilitator, disputants often do not listen to one another. Here are some self-inflicted impediments to active listening (Karrass, 1993):

- People think before they speak.
- People have lots on their minds that can't be switched off at a moment's notice.
- We tend to talk and interrupt too much.
- We are anxious to reframe and rebut the other person's arguments.
- We dismiss much of what we hear as irrelevant or uninteresting.
- We get distracted and lose concentration.
- We jump to conclusions before all of the facts are in.
- We tend to discard information we do not like.

Listening and Seeking to Understand Content and Feelings

Successful negotiators can engage in a collaborative process and listen to focus on information and facts presented by the other side. This is of vital importance in reaching resolution of conflicts in the workplace. The simple goal is to get and understand the information that is presented and convey to the other side that the message is understood. Successful conflict resolvers do not deny or ignore emotions; they identify and influence them.

In addition, listening for emotions and feelings can provide opportunities to demonstrate concern for grasping underlying emotions that the other side is attempting to convey. Empathic responses can indicate concern for feelings and these responses often invoke follow-up questions.

"How did that make you feel?"
"Why do you feel that way?"
"How does that work for you?"
"What do you see happening further down the road?"

In today's high-tech and high-speed world, communication is more important than ever, yet we seem to devote less and less time to really listening to one another. Genuine listening has become aligned with the gift of time. Face-to-face listening helps build relationships, solve problems, ensure understanding, resolve conflicts, and improve accuracy. At the workplace effective listening means fewer errors and less wasted time.

One good listening exercise that can be accomplished in the workplace within a small team or department is called "paraphrase."

Each of us interprets verbal information differently. The object of the paraphrase activity is to see how well participants summarize information as it is presented to them. A facilitator reads a short story and chooses a participant to paraphrase the story. Several employees should get the chance to paraphrase different stories. After each summary, other employees can give their personal interpretations of what they heard.

When employees feel fear during a workplace conflict, it is the largest obstacle that will inhibit listening whenever such disagreements or conflicts exist. People tend to be afraid that if they set their own perspectives aside for a moment and truly strive to understand another person's point of view they may be perceived to agree with others, even if no agreement exists. Some individuals might believe that they might not get a chance for their own point of view to be heard.

Who looks outside, dreams.
Who looks inside, awakens. ~ Carl Jung

There are many indications inherent in a person's conversation that can act as signposts to help follow what we're listening to. Discerning important content is vital in conflict discussions and we can be aided in understanding what a speaker is talking about when key phrases and words are uttered. For example, if an employee states, "I am going to explain three issues I have affecting my participation in this project," during that discussion one might hear the phrases *"first of all," "next"* and *"in summary"* to indicate the last part of the issues with participation. Therefore, when listening for details and information that is critical, one can focus on specific items that can provide the needed details.

Nonverbal Listening

Nonverbal communication includes facial expressions, the tone and pitch of the voice, gestures displayed through body language (*kinesics*) and the physical distance between the communicators (*proxemics*). These nonverbal signals can give clues and additional information and meaning over and above spoken (verbal) communication. While the key to success in professional relationships lies in one's ability to communicate well, it's not the words that we use but our nonverbal cues or "body language" that speak the loudest.

Professor emeritus of psychology Albert Mehrabian (1971) conducted a series of studies on communication, through which he developed what is now referred to as the "7–38–55 Rule." We focus mainly on words when we listen, however, on topics where we have invested emotional energy, like in conflict situations, most of our communication might be related nonverbally.

> Around 55 percent of human communication is relayed nonverbally. Nonverbal communication, which can include body messages, facial communication, and spatial communication can alter or affect what the other side thinks about what is being uttered.
>
> Some 38 percent of communication is conveyed in a person's tone of voice (the quality and resonance of the voice, the volume and pacing).
>
> A mere 7 percent of what we communicate on matters of emotional concern is contained in the words of the message themselves.

The nonverbal elements in communication indicate a person's feelings and opinions. When someone says something, their body language and intonation could be dominant, and there is no agreement between what they say and what they radiate. Apart from interaction, communication is also about the fact that the verbal and nonverbal elements support one another and that these are congruent. What someone says will then be more powerful and convincing because of their gestures and intonation. The message will absolutely be more unconvincing when there is no congruence and the receiver could be set on the wrong track. He will unconsciously focus more on the nonverbal elements that will always dominate collectively.

Negotiation and Ethics

In business and industry, the three big initials are R-O-I. The Return on Investment (ROI) is a performance measure used to evaluate the efficiency of an investment or compare the efficiency of several different investments. ROI measures the amount of return on an investment relative to the investment's cost. To calculate ROI, the benefit (or return) of an investment is divided by the cost of the investment. The result is expressed as a percentage or a ratio. The ROI calculation is flexible and can be manipulated for different uses. A company may use the calculation to compare the ROI on different potential investments, while an investor could use it to calculate a return on a stock. ROI is one of the most used profitability ratios because of its flexibility. One of the downsides of the ROI calculation is that it can be manipulated, so results may vary between users. Flexibility and manipulating ROI results can yield varying results. How about manipulation of other concerns in business?

Oscar Wilde once said, "the truth is rarely pure and never simple." Much has been written about business ethics, and recent years have produced well-publicized cases of manipulation (Bernard L. Madoff Investment Securities, Ivan Boesky and insider trading on Wall Street, Michael Milken of Drexel Burnham Lambert, Kenneth Lay of Enron, and Dennis Kozlowski of Tyco). When it comes to negotiation, and where information is everything, some individuals operate fast and loose with facts, figures, promises, and proposals. They may tell you what you *want* to hear, but not necessarily what you deserve to hear (Volkema, 1999).

Ethics, ethical behavior, and taking personal responsibility for choices carry even more importance in today's business world. Here are four basic ideas for consideration (Bucaro, 2016).

1. **What role does common good play in our decision making?**

It is of the utmost importance to be truly "other focused" as a central factor in maintaining ethical balance. Whether it is among us, as business professionals, or in dealing with our customers, staff, etc., the question that needs to be asked is "What can I do for you to get you to cooperate with me?"

2. **What is the importance of communal wisdom?**

Frank Bucaro believes that we sometimes tend to be too narrowly focused to see a bigger picture. There is a tendency, on occasion, to see our way as the only way or our approach as the only approach. We need to be open to others' perspectives, their honesty, and their genuine concern for us and our success. Any number of ethical issues, questions, and situations might easily be resolved by "tapping" the wisdom of those who have your best interest at heart. It certainly will cut the "learning curve" and keep you better focused on your task.

3. **Stay true to oneself and your values.**

The journey of life to this point has instilled in us our perceptions, attitudes, values and insights that have directed us as individuals and have been instrumental in the building of our businesses.

If that journey has been one of positive influence, we must stay true to it. However, if our journey has had some negative influences, we will be challenged to determine whether that's the path we want to follow or if we need an attitude check that may lead us to a more productive path.

4. **Always beware of the ethics gap.**

What is the ethics gap? It is what we know about right from wrong and what we think it takes to be successful. This gap is present in any situation, especially business. It's involved in how we work with customers, colleagues, staff, and even family. We need to align our work values and principles with their personal values and principles and proceed accordingly.

Smart Negotiators

How you behave during negotiation can have a dramatic impact on the outcome. Certain principles are always at play in the negotiation process and will help achieve your goals. Several key strategies are as follows: (1) Get the other side to commit first. Skilled negotiators realize that you're usually better off if you can get the other side to commit to a position first; (2) Act dumb, not smart. Sometimes, when you are negotiating, you're better off pretending you know less than everybody else does, not more than they do; (3) Concentrate on the issues. Negotiators know that they should always focus on the issues and not be distracted by the actions of the other negotiators; and (4) Validate and congratulate the other side. When you're finished negotiating, you should always validate and congratulate the other side (Lewicki, Barry, and Saunders, 2007).

There are many pitfalls, ploys, and tactics used during negotiation. Some of the most common, and most reported on, are (1) good cop, bad cop, (2) nibbles, (3) cherry-picking, and (4) take it or leave it. When negotiators employ these, they are attempting to undercut good intentions and often use sympathy or power tactics to get what they want. Knowing how to cope with these ploys are what makes smart negotiators smart. Two of the failures that smart negotiators never embrace are being inadequately prepared and failing to properly frame the issues.

The pitfalls and sneaky tactics mentioned above are used by individuals who try to gain an advantage over their counterparts. In place of outright lying and half-truths, smart negotiators, managers and team leaders can try the following solid alternatives.

Faced With...	Employ Instead...
1. Threats	1. Take time-outs to cool off. Suggest outside third-party assistance.
2. Fake issues	2. Propose new issues with real value.
3. Little concession movement	3. Commit to addressing other side's interest. Commit to standards.
4. Unverifiable facts	4. Focus on your uncertainty. Frame your facts carefully. State your opinion.
5. Seeking to determine your bottom line	5. Inquire about their bottom line. Speak factually about your goals.
6. Unwillingness to foster alternatives	6. Initiate efforts to propose alternatives. Highlight opportunities for agreement.
7. Phony or outrageous intentions	7. Stick to your game plan.
8. Getting caught unaware	8. Anticipate the issues of the other side in your original planning sessions. Base reactions and responses on what you know about the needs of the other side.

Negotiation Obstacles and Deal Killers

In his book *Never Split the Difference: Negotiating as If Your Life Depended on It*, Chris Vogel (2016) states that it is of critical importance to identify and diffuse deal-killing issues. This is especially significant with internal negotiations. Changes that may occur after a negotiated settlement may make the disputants look as if they have not been totally devoted to their job. The dilemma for the internal conflict resolver is how to make them look good in the face of change.

When negotiations get bogged down and the possibility of a no-deal situation looms, it is very effective to explore potential roadblocks with questions like (1) What do we seem up against here? (2) Can you help me understand the biggest challenge you face? (3) How will making a resolution affect the workplace? (4) What will happen if we do not settle? (5) How will moving to a settlement resonate with the company standards and practices?

All negotiations, whether internal or external, are unique, and creating and mixing the right questions to focus and drive the bargaining phase will allow the participants to open up about what their needs and wants are and will allow them to frame their point of views on the issues. Negotiations cannot result in agreements if one or both sides maintain steadfast inflexibility with respect to terms and conditions. Each disputant will desire to obtain certain concessions or items. However, the whole point of the negotiation process is to discuss how each side can give and take certain things so that a balance is struck. Unwillingness to compromise will certainly stall the negotiations and may preclude completion of the process altogether.

Deal killers, or deal breakers, are important if (1) they do not align with your needs; (2) they do not serve your purpose; (3) the other party requests resources or information you do not have access to; and (4) you do not feel instinctually good about them.

What About Mediation?

People in conflict have several procedural options to choose from to resolve their differences. Disagreements and problems that arise can usually be handled informally. Initially, people may *avoid* each other because they dislike the discomfort that accompanies conflict, they do not consider the issue to be that important, they lack the power to force a change, they do not believe the situation can be improved, or they are not yet ready to negotiate (Moore, 2003). When a dispute arises in an organization, some parties believe that arbitration or litigation is called for. The outcomes of decisions from these two conflict resolution methods take the control of decision-making out of the hands of the parties in dispute. When people cannot sit down and negotiate a dispute or conflict on their own, they may reach out to a neutral third party who will facilitate, not provide, some resolution. The opportunity to pursue mediation to resolve conflicts and facilitate settlements exists in many organizational endeavors.

The use and practice of mediation has grown significantly in many countries and cultures, but it has grown most rapidly in the United States and Canada. Mediation was first formally institutionalized in the U.S. in the area of labor-management relations (Simkin, 1971). The U.S. Department of Labor was established in 1913 with a panel of commissioners of conciliation that was tasked with handling conflicts between labor and management. This panel subsequently became the U.S. Conciliation Service and in 1947 was renamed as the Federal Mediation and Conciliation Service. The hope and desire of these groups was that mediated settlements would prevent costly strikes and that the welfare and wealth of Americans would be improved. The private sector also initiated labor-management and commercial relations mediation.

The American Arbitration Association (AAA) was founded in 1926 by the merger of the Arbitration Society of America and the Arbitration Foundation to provide dispute resolution and avoid court proceedings. The AAA (2005) established model standards of conduct of mediators. The preamble to these standards state:

> Mediation is used to resolve a broad range of conflicts within a variety of settings. These Standards are designed to serve as fundamental ethical guidelines for persons mediating in all practice contexts. They serve three primary goals: to guide the conduct of mediators; to inform the mediating parties; and to promote public confidence in mediation as a process for resolving disputes. Mediation is a process in which an impartial third party facilitates communication and negotiation and promotes voluntary decision making by the parties to the dispute. Mediation serves various purposes, including providing the opportunity for parties to define and clarify issues, understand different perspectives, identify interests, explore and assess possible solutions, and reach mutually satisfactory agreements, when desired.

When negotiation fails it may be because human communication has gone off-center. Three reasons (Fisher and Brown, 1988) negotiation may fail include (1) we assume there is no need to talk, (2) we communicate in one direction, and (3) we send mixed messages. A general strategy to overcome these barriers has three components: (1) always consult and engage in fact-finding, (2) open up to listening actively, and (3) plan and clarify the communication process to minimize misunderstandings. When, and if, these fail or fall short, mediation might be the answer.

A variety of mediators can be found in organizational culture (Moore, 2003).

- Social Network Mediator
- Benevolent Mediator
- Administrative/Managerial Mediator
- Vested Interest Mediator
- Independent Mediator

Mediators can adopt three approaches (Griffith and Goodwin, 2016): facilitative, evaluative, and transformative. Facilitative mediation is focused on supporting the process of communication and decision-making between the parties and less involved in evaluating the merits of the issues. The mediator engages in reflective listening skills to ensure each party is fully heard and fully understands the other party's views and positions. Evaluative mediation is a process whereby the mediator facilitates communication between the parties and leaves decision making in the hands of the disputants. An evaluative mediator is more involved in offering possible solutions for resolution and in offering insights on the merits of the parties' positions and proposals. Transformative mediation is also concerned with facilitating an effective communication process but has a broader focus in supporting the parties' ongoing relationship. The mediators encourage each party to give recognition and understanding to the other party's perspective.

In a nutshell, mediation is the involvement of an impartial third party to support and help those involved in a conflict to find a resolution. The key difference between negotiation and mediation is that in negotiation, the parties involved work out their own agreement. In mediation, they have the support of the third party, the mediator, to help them come to an agreement. Mediation, whether formal or informal, can often help solve conflicts that have gone beyond the negotiation stage. Although much research indicates that mediation if effective in many conflicts, parties are often reticent to try it because they are unfamiliar with the process and distrustful of their adversary. In some organizations, mediation may be unavailable, but forward-thinking companies have instituted training programs to bring mediation services to their employees. Typical settings for mediation services are human resources departments or ombudsperson offices. Managers can be given training to empower them to intervene directly in conflict between subordinates.

Managing disputes with the assistance of a mediator will eventually be a cost-cutting measure for an organization that may have to look for and engage in litigation. Key highlights of organizational mediation are (1) the workforce members in dispute agree to voluntarily participate; (2) there are face-to-face discussions involving an unbiased mediator without any decision-making power; (3) mediators assist the employees to understand each other's point of view and come to an agreement; (4) equal opportunities exist for the disputants to speak and explain their perspective; (5) all relevant information is shared; and (6) agreements are laser-focused on shared outcomes that are satisfactory to the disputants.

The agreements reached through mediation should be SMART—that is, Specific, Measurable, Attainable, Realistic and Time-bound.

I served as a member of the first educational consortium to be trained in mediation by the International Center for Cooperation and Conflict Resolution (ICCCR) at Teachers College, Columbia University, with the collaboration of Ellen Raider (ICCCR) and Alan Borer (New York City Board of Education). We were trained to become "turn-key trainers" to establish peer mediation programs/centers in our secondary schools. The most memorable sections of that training focused on the *phase characteristics* of mediation (ICCCR, 2009).

Beginning Phase
- Set the context
- Build warm climate
- Establish rapport
- Identify influencing factors for both parties
- Think about problem-solving

Middle Phase
- Identify positions, issues
- Probe for the needs of both parties (psychological and tangible)
- Probe toward problem-solving
- Paraphrase at the content and feelings level
- Use active listening
- Develop a reframe at the needs level and transition to end phase

End Phase
- Reaffirm reframing of issues to needs level
- Apply creativity toward resolving the conflict
- Use brainstorming to identify all possibilities
- Decide on mutually beneficial agreement

Any training program aimed at developing negotiation and mediation facilitators at the workplace includes an interactive approach encompassing several days. Several training modules could be structured as (1) an overview of the conflict resolution process; (2) development of structural models of the elements of negotiation and mediation; (3) communication behaviors used in negotiation and mediation; (4) examination of cultural differences affecting the conflict resolution process; and (5) dealing with emotional and cross-cultural aspects of conflict resolution.

The Morton Deutsch International Center for Cooperation and Conflict Resolution (MDICCR) situated at Teachers College, Columbia University in New York City is one of many institutions that offer training and certification in negotiation and mediation. MDICCR offers a wide range of courses for scholar-practitioners in the areas of cooperation, conflict resolution, dynamic systems, and social justice. It develops and provides state-of-the-art instruction, training, and professional development for students, practitioners, educators, and organizational leaders.

Training and education objectives include opportunities to develop the fundamental skills required to be successful practitioners of cooperation and conflict resolution: self-reflection and awareness; communication regarding needs and objectives; negotiation and mediation. Another objective leads to the development of future leaders who will further the development of theory and practice in the interrelated areas of conflict resolution, cooperation, and social justice. Lastly, the training will increase public awareness of constructive methods for conflict prevention and resolution of many forms of oppression, of strategies for overcoming social injustice in families, organizations, and communities worldwide, and for fostering sustainable peace.

Course work, trainings, and workshops can include Basic Practicum in Negotiation and Conflict Resolution; Standard and Adaptive Mediation Skills; Fundamentals of Cooperation and Conflict Resolution; Conflict and Complexity; Healing and Reconciling Relationships; Transforming Conflict from Within; and Managing Conflicts in Organizations.

Another institution that can offer training and certification in the areas of conflict resolution is the John Jay College of Criminal Justice in New York City. The Dispute Resolution Certificate program provides opportunities to learn about the causes, complex dynamics, escalation, de-escalation, and constructive resolution of conflicts in a variety of contexts, from the interpersonal to the international levels. Learners also gain knowledge and techniques necessary to negotiate, facilitate, and mediate a wide range of situations.

The Society of Professionals in Dispute Resolution (SPIDR) is an independent, non-profit distributing and a non-governmental professional membership organization. SPIDR conducts research and evaluation programs including the setting of world class standards for mediation, arbitration and all practitioners in the field of alternative dispute resolution (ADR). It also helps to engage and empower dispute resolution professionals and practitioners, maintain a register of neutrals, including admission thereto and removal therefrom. The organization has over the years provided tools and support to workers, managers, organizations, government offices and officials, and others with regard to the resolution of disputes.

SPIDR has developed quality assessment programs that create methodologies for evaluating mediators. The criteria they are looking at are relationship, process and content skills. Relationship skills denote that applicants must be able to create an environment conducive to mediation and to develop communication and interaction with each individual participant. Process skills point to the ability to establish and maintain an effective working structure and manage the process and work through the phases of mediation. Content skills focus on the capability to facilitate the parties in creating workable solutions and enable momentum and progress through active engagement with the parties and the content of the dispute.

In 2001, SPIDR merged with two other organizations, the Academy of Family Mediators and the Conflict Resolution Education Network (CREnet), to form the Association for Conflict Resolution (ACR), the largest mediation and dispute resolution organization in the United States. Individuals and organizations that would like to investigate what these organizations offer can find more information at www.acrnet.org.

Third-Party Assistance/Arbitration

When efforts at mediation, with a neutral third party, fail despite the best efforts of a mediator, an organization may call in a trained arbitrator to settle the dispute. Arbitration is a form of alternative dispute resolution (ADR) and is one way to resolve disputes outside the courts when litigation is not always the answer. Companies are often intimidated by and reluctant to take on the financial burden that can come with the legal process of trials, not to mention the apprehension of not knowing for certain how a jury will decide until the very end.

Arbitration is different from mediation because the neutral arbitrator has the authority to decide about the dispute. The arbitration process is like a trial in that the parties make opening statements and present evidence to the arbitrator. Compared to traditional trials, arbitration usually takes less time and is less formal. In most cases third-party assistance is used in organizations with a unionized work force and the disputes concern labor-management issues.

A third-party arbitrator might be called in if the situation between the parties is volatile. Another reason is the breakdown of communication to the extent that individuals exhibit negative behaviors that may be manifested in intense anger, name-calling, bullying and verbal threats. Often differences in interests appear to be irreconcilable and the disputants believe that there are no established procedures for resolving the conflict or that procedures have not been followed. Arbitrators will be needed if the negotiations have completely broken down and there is an impasse (Moore, 1996).

Lewicki, Hiam and Olander (1996) have outlined some advantages and disadvantages of using arbitration to settle disputes.

1a. A clear solution is made available to the parties.
1b. The parties relinquish control over shaping the proposed solution or outcome.
2a. The solution may be mandated.
2b. The parties may not like the outcome and it may impose additional burdens on them.
3a. Arbitrators are selected because they are fair and impartial.
3b. If the arbitration is voluntary, the parties may lose face if they decide not to follow the arbitrator's recommendation.
4a. The costs of prolonging the dispute are avoided.
4b. There is a *decision-acceptance effect*: there is less commitment to an arbitrated resolution because the parties didn't participate in shaping the outcome, and the recommended settlement may be inferior to what they preferred.

Arbitration	Mediation
Arbitrator decides the matter.	Disputants select mediator and decide the matter.
Less expensive than litigation, but more expensive than mediation.	Less expensive than litigation or arbitration.
Relationships may become strained.	Relationships are likely to be maintained.
Usually a binding resolution.	Parties shape the resolution.
Could be win-lose outcome.	Usually a win-win outcome.
Adversarial components.	Collaborative components.
Resolution based on facts, evidence, company policies, procedures, and laws.	Resolution based on the needs of the parties.
Definite closure.	Uncertain closure.

Types of Arbitration Used by Organizations

In a report on the widespread use of arbitration among American companies, Professor Szalai and Judge Wessel (2018) of the Loyola University New Orleans College of Law have listed several arbitration cases and the nature of the conflicts:

State Farm Insurance	Wage and Hour Violations
PepsiCo	Wrongful Termination
UPS	Age Discrimination
FedEx	Race and Gender Discrimination
Nationwide	Unfair Trade Practices
Oracle	Breach of Contract
Wells Fargo	Disability Discrimination
General Motors	Whistleblower Retaliation
American Express	Violation of Family Medical Leave Act

For certain types of disputes, the authors postulate "arbitration can be a reasonable forum, provided that there is meaningful consent, fair procedures, and no significant public interest in the particular dispute."

However, with employment disputes, meaningful consent is frequently lacking, and the arbitration clause may be loaded with harsh, one-sided terms favoring an employer. Moreover, there is a strong societal interest in robust public enforcement of critical employment laws, like civil rights laws and wage laws. Employers should not be able to rig the game against workers and conceal wrongdoing using harsh, one-sided arbitration clauses hidden in the fine print.

7

Confrontational Innovation and Design

Common Design Thinking Tenets

Design thinking is a human-centered approach to innovation that draws from the designer's toolkit to integrate the needs of people, the possibilities of technology, and the requirements for business success. Design is a concept most often used to describe a product, an object or an end result. Design thinking takes that up a notch by offering a protocol for solving existing problems and uncovering new opportunities. In essence, the design thinking process is iterative, flexible and focused on collaboration between designers and users, with an emphasis on bringing ideas to life based on how real users think, feel and behave. Design thinking tackles complex problems by understanding human needs and defining problems in human-centric ways.

Conflict, crisis, and confrontation often occur together. None are very pleasant, but all three are part of our working environment. We have observed that there are differing views on the best way to manage conflict, but there is consensus that every situation is different.

Organization leaders who exhibit a willingness to support the teaching of design thinking skills to their workforce soon become aware of the benefits derived from design thinking's use as a conflict management tool. This includes paying more attention to the development of communication and conflict skills that support its success. Thomas Lockwood (2009) points out in his book *Design Thinking* that several tenets appear to be common in design thinking and found in design thinking organizations. Design thinking organizations seek to identify the right problem to solve, employing empathy that is coupled with collaboration through the formulation of multi-disciplinary teams. Learning is accelerated through hands-on experimentation and visualization with an integration of business model innovations during the process of design thinking, rather than adding it later or using it to limit creative ideation.

Handling confrontations in the workplace involves (1) talking with the other person, (2) focusing on the behavior and events, not on personalities, (3) listening carefully to identify points of agreement and disagreement, and (4) prioritizing the areas of conflict to develop a plan to work on each conflict.

Fear of confrontations at the workplace are often based on false assumptions. Thoughts like "This situation is bad" or "Telling my workmate that I disagree with them will ruin our relationship" will only exacerbate any fears. Confrontation, like conflict, is healthy. Facing and dealing with these issues can give rise to resolution, agreement and personal satisfaction.

Leaders and managers in organizations can succeed in dealing with confrontations and guide their employees through conflict and crisis. Without diving into frustration and chaos over confrontations, success can be achieved by following the three Q's:

Question: Question and diagram the confrontational situation quickly to determine the root of the issue.
Quiz: Ask the employee(s) to explain the facts as they view them. This will highlight what the root(s) of the problem are.
Quantify: Make connections to the facts, the goals and values of the organization, and take appropriate action to fix or modify the situation to make improvements.

Engagement and Confrontation

Dan Tapscott (2009) writes that in physics, the smallest particle into which a substance can be divided and still have the identity of the original substance is the molecule. Molecules are held together by electrical forces. He says they are "in a sense, networked, and the molecule is a good analogy for the optimal role of the Net Gen knowledge worker in today's digital economy."

Employees who are networked have replaced the original corporate hierarchy as the optimal structure of an organization as a vehicle of profit and wealth creation. Employment is a relationship between the employee and the employer and it needs commitment and collaboration from both sides. When confrontation or conflict occurs, the employer needs to engage in conflict management approaches that ensure a long-term collaboration that will last throughout a worker's career, at every stage of the employee life cycle.

Conflict resolution strategies in today's companies and today's workforce are changing the ways we should think about talent and work. Tapscott highlights the following guidelines for company managers that may alleviate organizational confrontations: (1) rethink recruitment and instead initiate relationships; (2) rethink training and engage in lifelong learning to strengthen all components of all jobs; and (3) rethink retention and evolve lasting relationships.

Types of Dissent

Expressing dissent is usually a sign that employees begin to disagree or have contradictory opinions about the company, its policies and practices. This expression of dissent may be an important practice because it provides workers with a way to deal with organizational constraints, draw attention to an overlooked issue, expose unethical behavior or illegal wrongdoing and provide corrective feedback (Waldron & Kassing, 2011). This dissenting confrontation may be triggered by an event that workers find disturbing or unsettling, such as the ways in which employees are treated, the way performance appraisals are conducted, or the implementation of changes to the working environment.

The ways employees express their dissent can be catalogued as upward, latent or displaced (Kassing, 1998).

UPWARD DISSENT	Voicing concerns directly and openly with supervisors because they feel that their concerns will be taken seriously.
LATENT DISSENT	Sharing concerns aggressively with coworkers rather than with management. They feel their dissent possesses little value and their contributions are unwanted.
DISPLACED DISSENT	Discussing work-related concerns with people outside the organization. They are complaints and frustrations employees aren't eager to share with superiors because they fear retaliation.

Difficult Conversations

Having uncomfortable conversations at work is never easy, whether it's with subordinates or coworkers. This is especially true for people who are afraid of conflict and would do anything possible to avoid it. Sidestepping difficult conversations can lead to dysfunction and lack of performance, which can ultimately have a negative impact on a team and the business. Workplace conflict affects not only morale and productivity, but also turnover.

Confrontation suggests meeting someone face to face that may have some hostile intent. How can this difficult conversation create value for the parties involved and for the organization? Fit is important to get clear on the intention/desired outcome. The conversation must be focused objectively and include both insights and opportunities to improve.

There are several types of difficult workplace conversations you might find yourself having at some point during your career. Here are some examples:

- Behavior issues
- Interpersonal conflict issues
- Policy violations
- External partner complaints
- Excessive absences
- Insubordination
- Customer/client complaints
- Coworker complaints

Difficult conversations challenge employees because they involve a lot of button-pushing. It is normal for people to get defensive or start panicking when they feel they're "in trouble" with their supervisor. Difficult conversations need to address behavior, not an assessment of their behavior. Confrontation using inferences like "irresponsible" or "not a team player" causes defensiveness and makes success less likely. It is better to ask, "What is the evidence for my inference?" and confront based on that behavior. That's why it's important to project a sense of calm fairness, not anger or judgment.

Difficult conversations can have three underlying structures (Stone, Patton & Heen, 2010) that can be labeled as the *What Happened?* conversation; the *Feelings* conversation; and the *Identity* conversation. In the *What Happened?* conversation participants disagree on who said or did what. *The Feelings* conversation is directed at acknowledging feelings you or the other side exhibited and determining if they are valid or not. In the *Identity* conversation there is an examination of what the conflict situation means which may lead to an internal debate over self-image, self-esteem and the future of relationships in the organization.

To assist with the examination, discussion and resolution of conflicts, using an I-message or I-statement is beneficial. This is an assertion about the feelings, beliefs, values, etc., of the person speaking, generally expressed as a sentence beginning with the word "I" and contrasted with a "you-message" or "you-statement," which often begins with the word "You" and focuses on the person spoken to. I-messages are often used with the intent to be assertive without putting the other side on the defensive. They are also used to take ownership for one's feelings rather than implying that they are caused by another person.

Many communication researchers view I-statements as a dispute resolution conversation opener that can be used to state how one sees things and how one would like things to be, without using inflammatory language. Using the first-person singular pronoun is a great way to cement boundaries without escalating into confrontations. When you state, "I'm sorry, that kind of thinking doesn't work for me," the word "I" purposefully fixes the other side's attention onto you long enough for you to proceed and make your point.

First, describe the behavior by using "When I hear you say…" Then explain the feelings or thoughts it creates: "I feel/think …" Then note the effect their behavior has: "It impacts…" I-messages promote a willingness to find a solution and seek constructive change without conflict.

I-Message

I FEEL _____

(tell the other person how you feel, using an emotional term)

WHEN _____

(describe the specific event that caused you to feel this way)

PLEASE _____

(explain what you would like to happen in the future)

Competencies to Handle Confrontation

Many of us have been on the receiving end of confrontations in the workplace. Sometimes we do not handle it well, and many times we can't single out what went wrong. Initially, we want to treat everyone, the team or department and the confronter, with the utmost respect. Most people are sincere in their beliefs and have what they consider good reasons for holding them. The confrontational person is usually an intelligent, thoughtful human being and should be taken seriously.

Here are some competencies that should be developed to deal with a confrontational crisis:

- Is the basic issue one that relies on trust, promise and/or workplace commitments?
- Is the issue focused on authoritarian procedures?
- Does open communication exist? And if not, why not?
- Is the confrontation about an ignored conflict?
- Does feedback or lack of feedback contribute to the confrontation?
- Are the company's efforts at collaboration and independence part of the issue?
- Is the main problem a lack of support and cooperation from workmates?
- Is the issue couched in vague or unknown problems and actions?

To confront and resolve a confrontational person, one should attempt to learn as much as possible about him or her to anticipate challenges. It will also aid in avoiding unpleasant surprises. Additionally, and as important as knowing the confronter, one will need to understand and work through one's own feelings about the subject matter of the confrontation as well as one's feelings about those who hold opposing views. It is key to understand how one feels and responds when confronted by an angry or arrogant person. Anger is a powerful emotion.

In some confrontational situations, anger triggers the fight/flight response, which mentally and physically prepares the body for survival. During the flight/flight response, the body automatically responds to a threat without conscious thought. As the threat increases, a person's ability to reason diminishes. Angry people experience the same phenomenon, because anger is a reaction to a real or perceived threat. Confrontational people often talk and act without thinking. The level of cognitive impairment depends on the intensity of the anger and these individuals are not open to solutions.

Breaking the confrontation cycle allows people to vent their anger and provides them with a course of action they have a hard time refusing. The greatest effort to break this cycle involves utilizing empathic statements. Most people would agree that showing empathy is much more about action than it is about words. Empathic statements can capture a person's verbal message, physical status, or emotional feeling, and using parallel language, reflect those feelings back to that person.

Confrontational people may often struggle with vulnerability because they have been burned before or simply ignored. They may not want to share their struggles for fear that they won't receive an empathetic response. So when a workmate chooses to open up to you, even in a confrontational manner, it indicates that he or she really trusts you. It's your job to honor that and respond with care and appreciation. The bottom line of how we respond to a confrontation has nothing to do with the attacker. It has to do with who we are and how we choose to behave.

Such rephrasing helps you maintain control of the discussion and avoid being manipulated. You reveal hidden assumptions and possible absurdities in your attacker's position. You also make the confronter responsible for the content of the question, while at the same time demonstrating that you're taking the question, and the questioner, seriously. And finally, you gain a better understanding of the question, and perhaps discover a productive line of response in the process.

Empathy Statements

- I am sorry to see that you are in this situation.
- I can see how this is important to you.
- I know how this can be confusing.
- I understand how this can be frustrating.
- Let's see if we can resolve this together.

Unmanageable Levels of Confrontation

One of the reasons confrontations reach unmanageable levels and resolution and accord are not reached is because leaders and employees tend to personalize the experience. When others challenge an individ-

- Has a clear focus been defined and effectively communicated throughout the organization?

What Hartman and LeGrande have learned is that "ruthless execution means that business leaders take the time and opportunity to study the issues—and then act on them. During tough times, leaders do not have to rush into making decisions, but just the opposite. They have predefined strategic and operational methodologies that allow them to uncover issues early and react prudently, focusing the company's efforts to drive through the wall."

Google will need to exhibit patience for making decisions in uncertain times, because the last thing organizations aspire to do is to suggest that it is easy to revitalize the company.

Dismissal and Termination

Dismissal and termination may be one way to deal with a confrontational worker. Dismissal is when the employer chooses to require the employee to leave, generally for a reason which is the fault of the employee. Termination is an employee's departure from a job and the end of an employee's duration with an employer. Termination carries a stigma in many cultures and may hinder the jobseeker's chances of finding new employment, particularly if he or she has been terminated from a previous job. Termination normally entails wrongdoing on the part of the employee, while dismissal is punishment for a delinquent employee. Termination is the end of a contract, where there are no benefits for the employee while there may be some benefits allowed by the management in the case of dismissal.

Many organizations have developed assessment policies for working with a troublesome employee. HR professionals can play an integral role in providing guidance and training to managers with difficult employees. HR should adopt the role of business partner and help managers look at the presenting issue and uncover the underlying issue. A critical step is getting the manager to recognize that a problem exists.

Leaders often avoid dealing with interpersonal issues because these problems can be very difficult and complicated to resolve. HR professionals can assist leaders in identifying problems and strategizing possible solutions for confrontational or troublesome workers. One HR assessment is the 360 Assessment. Organizations use a variety of methods to seek 360 feedback about employees. Some are more common than others, and that may depend upon the culture and climate of the organization.

The 360 Assessment is a professional feedback opportunity that enables a group of coworkers to provide feedback on an employee's performance. Coworkers who participate in the 360 review usually include the employee's supervisor, several peers, reporting staff members, and functional managers with whom the employee works regularly. The objective of the feedback is to give the employee the opportunity to understand how their work is viewed in the total organization.

Behaviors exhibited by confrontational, conflicted, or troubled employees can indicate a need for some type of intervention before dismissal or termination is enacted. Knapp, Vangelisti and Caughlin (2014) list the following characteristic behaviors that are toxic to workmates, managers, and the organization: (1) increasing physical distance between workmates and increasing time between interactions; (2) shorter encounters with less personal information exchanged; (3) superlatives and absolute statements couched in negative rather than positive evaluations; and (4) an increasing concern for self rather than for the relationship.

Preparation for Taking Action

It is a good idea for organizations to work with employees at the hiring stage to lay the groundwork for them to understand their behavioral expectations as well as their job responsibilities. It is also ideal for managers to be prepared to act when employees fall short of those expectations. Basic training workshops, seminars and/or orientations in people management and conflict resolution can be a good starting place.

Many organizations offer in-house or outsourced people management programs. Some of these include the 360-degree assessments that help to gauge where the manager's people skills may need further development. Providing managers with support, including the tools they need to succeed, will help them feel more confident when confronted with difficult employees.

Facilitating meaningful teamwork activities can build better understanding between coworkers. More companies are now including civility training for all employees, which can include business etiquette, cultural sensitivity and diversity awareness components. Training need not only define civility and list the employer's expectations, it can teach what civility looks like and describe or act out scenarios ripe for incivility. This will give participants the opportunity to practice how to maintain composure instead of acting out (Society for Human Resource Management, 2018).

When preparing to take some action it is prudent to be aware that one of the main reasons employees engage in disruptive behaviors is because they don't feel they are being heard. When unacceptable behaviors appear, effective managers will start to pay close attention to what is going on and not turn away from problems they'd rather ignore.

1. Make note of specific behaviors to address, including when they were observed and who was present.
2. Take time to collect information and understand the issue as fully as possible.
3. Be sure to solicit the problematic employee's point of view; by doing so, managers often learn of something that is blocking the employee's progress and causing stress, which can be addressed and resolved. Just being heard can also be a factor in de-escalating negative behaviors before they get out of control.
4. Provide open and honest feedback.
5. Document and follow disciplinary policies.
6. Discuss appropriate behaviors with the employee and ensure that he or she understands what is expected in the future.
7. Communicate the organization's codes of conduct and labor agreements that contain requirements that employees and managers treat each other with dignity and respect and conduct themselves in a professional manner. (In addition, most organizations have policies that prohibit harassment and discrimination, including actions that may lead to an intimidating, hostile or offensive work environment.)

Management of Opportunities

Building an organization culture to effectively deal with confrontation and conflict is the goal of proactive, performance-driven, and relationship-oriented companies. This is a most challenging time where employees, team, department and division collaborations must permeate all transactions and business opportunities. Managing business ventures and opportunities cuts to the core of high-performance levels that helps create and sustain an organization's vision and mission.

cessfully deal with conflict and the human instinct to avoid it. Setting a balance allows us to embrace conflict to keep our focus on the organization's goals and provides individuals with an opportunity to visualize, accept, and clarify their goals and needs. Once we can embrace and address conflict, that is the time when we can establish, build and fortify *trust*.

Openness of the Manager

A conflict resolution process in an organization aimed at integrative (collaborative) solutions requires a manager who embodies a total sense of openness that reflects flexible and creative options. Griffith and Goodwin (2016) delineate six characteristics of an effective and open manager.

> *Problem solver*: Encouraging brainstorming and an examination of all possible options to resolution.
> *Risk taker*: Encouraging the consideration of options that may not have been considered before and that may move individuals beyond their comfort zones.
> *Comfort with uncertainty*: Working with disputants to seek answers and make connections that have not previously been explored.
> *Inventive*: Bringing up new proposals and ways of viewing things that help disputants overcome entrenched thinking.
> *Forward thinking*: Challenging everyone to opine about how various options will impact the parties in the long term.
> *Adaptive*: Compromise, compete, collaborate, or accommodate as warranted.

Management Productivity

When managers can achieve effective and explicit agreements, all those involved in resolving conflict should feel satisfied in their professional and personal relationships. Conflict managers who formulate collaborative agreements are those who can set and reach goals. These managers improve the quality of work and work relationships and that increases the level of trust at the workplace. Companies want to improve productivity and reduce and resolve conflicts. Many organizations exhibit a natural tendency to provide feedback to the workforce, and that is a grand thing.

Providing meaningful feedback in a constructive manner on a regular basis is a part of every conflict manager's approach to conflict resolution sessions. Feedback is a foundational management skill. Valued feedback and support can take many forms. Employee goodwill and loyalty are built by management support in times of conflict resolution sessions.

Key to organizational productivity is the capability of company managers to articulate expectations and ensure that the employees commit to them. Clarity in these expectations means they are behaviorally specific.

Productivity/efficiency: Uses work time effectively.

Time management: Manages workload; demonstrates ability to prioritize assignments by meeting routine and unexpected deadlines; handles multiple tasks and deadlines.

Meeting deadlines: Overcomes obstacles and roadblocks; commits fully to the job and deadlines; concentrates on outcomes.

Flexibility and adaptability: Adapts to changes quickly; can modify plans to meet changing organizational needs.

Decision making: Recognizes when to make independent decisions and when to consult supervisors.

Innovation/future oriented: Actively applies new knowledge skills; seeks additional training.

Critical thinking: Capitalizes on, contributes to and identifies opportunities to increase work productivity.

Managerial behavior frequently is determined by situational factors, such as the organization in which a person operates. When organizational practices are so fixed and rigid as to permit only small variations in individual behavior, the management style exhibited may reflect little of a person's own thinking. Various management styles and assumptions may depend upon the situation, values, personality and chance (Natemeyer & Hersey, 2011).

- *Situation*—This can be the determining factor dictating which set of managerial assumptions are employed. Management of people in the crisis of a conflict situation is likely to be different than it would be under routine circumstances.
- *Values*—An individual's choice of managerial assumptions may be based upon values that he or she holds concerning the "right" way to treat people or the way to manage to achieve best results.
- *Personality*—The dominant management style may result from deep-rooted personality characteristics which predispose an individual to prefer one approach over another.

ager will embrace and possess outstanding facilitation skills. To lead these sessions and provide order and coherence to the statements and contributions the disputants make, Silberman (2006) prescribes the following:

> *Paraphrase* what someone has said so they know they have been understood.
> *Check* your understanding against the words of the participant or ask them to clarify what they said.
> *Compliment* an insightful comment.
> *Energize* the discussion by prodding the parties for more elaboration on their contributions.
> *Mediate* differences and insist on limiting interruptions.
> *Collate* and pull together items of common ground that can become parts of an agreement.
> *Summarize* frequently what has transpired to keep the individuals on track.

Effective leader facilitation creates an inclusive environment where everyone is clear about the expectations and intentions among all parties. Everyone must understand that enough time will be provided for disputants to gather their thoughts and plan their positions and viewpoints. Managers understand that not all of the parties will have the same expectations for how the session will proceed.

Managers and Critical Thinking

Critical thinking is self-guided, self-disciplined thinking that attempts to reason at the highest level of quality in a fair-minded way. Leaders who think critically develop an awareness of the concepts and principles that enable them to analyze, assess, and improve their thinking. They work to develop the intellectual virtues of intellectual integrity, intellectual humility, intellectual civility, intellectual empathy, intellectual sense of justice and confidence in reason. It is these qualities that aid them in acting as conflict resolvers, negotiators or mediators in their organizations.

To avoid thinking simplistically about complicated issues these leaders recognize the complexities in developing as thinkers and commit themselves to a lifelong practice toward self-improvement and the self-improvement of their direct reports. Through critical thinking leaders/

managers can raise vital questions and problems and formulate them clearly and precisely. They can gather and assess relevant information open-mindedly within alternative systems of thought, recognizing and assessing, as need be, assumptions, implications, and practical consequences. Critical thinking enables communicators to interact effectively with employees and others in determining solutions to complex problems.

Some individuals believe that critical thinking may hamper creativity because it requires following rules of logic and rationality, but creativity might require breaking rules. This is a misconception. Critical thinking is quite compatible with thinking "out of the box," challenging consensus and pursuing less popular approaches. Effective company managers, administrators and supervisors understand the importance of out-of-the-box thinking. Here are several positive examples of critical thinking (Facione & Gittens, 2013).

1. A manager trying to be as objective as possible when settling a dispute by summarizing the alternatives, with fairness to all sides of a disagreement.
2. A team of scientists working with great precision through a complex experiment to gather and analyze data.
3. A person running a small business trying to anticipate the possible economic and human consequences of various ways to increase sales or reduce costs.
4. A safety engineer discovering lead in the company's water supply and working out a communication plan and resolution guide.
5. An educator using clever questioning to guide a student to new insights.
6. Police detectives, crime scene analysts, lawyers, judges, and juries systematically investigating and evaluating the evidence as they seek justice.
7. A financial planner anticipating the impact of new income tax legislation on a client's future tax liabilities.
8. A first responder coming upon the scene of an accident and quickly analyzing the situation, evaluating priorities, and inferring what actions to be taken and in what order.

The global knowledge economy is driven by information and technology. Organization leaders must be able to deal with changes quickly and effectively for the new economy places increasing demands on flexible intellectual skills and the ability to analyze information and integrate diverse sources of knowledge in solving problems. Superb critical thinking promotes such thinking skills and is very important in the fast-changing workplace.

Our values play a significant role in our thinking, logic and other cognitive functions. Workplace collaborations operate best when there are shared values among the workforce that encourage a respect for everyone's ideas. When individuals possess similar values, conflicts may be assuaged, not arise, or be easily ameliorated. Values acknowledged to be vital assets to critical thinking that managers should be aware of are (1) independent thinking; (2) empathy and humility; (3) integrity, perseverance and civility; (4) curiosity and imagination; and (5) responsibility and self-esteem.

When managers adjust and modify their awareness of the role that values play in their thinking process, they can quickly see what happens when certain values are lacking. This can certainly lead to employee disagreements and workplace conflicts. Employees who display arrogance, hostility and irresponsibility are hard to work with. These people are lacking certain values. In the following two examples, how would a conflict manager or conflict management team address the issues and concerns presented?

....

Dewey is a marketing director for a mid-sized pharmaceutical company. He discovered that the CEO was not telling the truth. At weekly meetings she would say things that sabotaged what she had said she wanted the marketing team to accomplish. Dewey sensed that she did not possess integrity and it became uncomfortable for him to continue working for someone he did not respect. He left the company.

....

Ellen is the COO of a collaborative software company and has an employee that is top-notch at remote installation. However, he can be arrogant and brusque to everyone around him. He has, on many occasions, mentioned that he is not really a team player and prefers to perform the work he was hired for by himself. Members of the installation team are met with sarcastic comments when they attempt to correct him. He is intimidating and has no sense of humor.

....

Managers as Change Agents

Change is the law of life, and those who look only to the past or present are certain to miss the future. ~ John F. Kennedy

One of the first experts to focus on the process of educational change was Ronald Havelock (1973). His concepts and ideas aimed at educational institutions can be easily interfaced with enterprise institutions. Havelock's linkage model of the change process is based on a systems perspective that zeroes in on two systems: the user system and the resource system. The user system is guided by the need to resolve a problem, while the resource system represents the source of information to guide the user in his or her efforts to solve the problem. Change agents are the individuals who facilitate the change process and guide users to solve problems.

Organizational managers, serving as these agents of change, participate by establishing constructive relationships among employees, while helping them identify problems and opportunities that might necessitate change. They encourage employees to communicate problems facing them or their team. They provide relevant resources to support the many aspects of the change process and work with employees to adopt change and to develop support for various initiatives. These managers stabilize the change and ensure that it is integrated into the structure of the organization, and treat everyone equally to avoid causing resentments.

Change management is no longer an idea that means only operational improvements and cost efficiencies. Change agents have become a more interwoven part of the overall company context. Change agents in the 21st century require the ability not only to continuously manage crisis and change, but also to see around and beyond the obvious in order to anticipate the unexpected before circumstances force one's hand. As managers and supervisors, people can never forget about the customers and clients that contribute to the growth of the business, and must never grow complacent about understanding their changing needs and demands.

Leaders are affected by consumer and competitive behaviors. Therefore, they must change the way that they view these behaviors, and, in many respects, leaders must become aware of how each part of the organization impacts them directly and indirectly so they can be more proactive in their thinking, planning and execution. Bridging the gap between what is happening and what is possible is what being an agent of change is all about. The traditional process for creating organizational change involves digging deep to uncover the root causes of problems, hiring experts or importing best-of-breed practices, and assigning a strong role to leaders as champions of change.

Most employees don't embrace change at the same pace. How managers communicate new ideas plays a huge role in how well they're received and how quickly they will be adopted. Change agents and innovators may be tempted to think that conveying enthusiasm and excitement will accelerate others' acceptance; that might not be the case all the time. What may be compelling to innovators and change agents may not be compelling to more pragmatic and conservative employees. Innovators are often in the small minority. Change agents advocate, encourage, facilitate, manage, and mediate organization change.

A large obstacle for managers to achieve win-win resolutions lies in inventing realistic options for each side's concerns in a conflict situation. Ury & Fisher (2001) explain that to invent creative options, managers will need to (1) separate the act of inventing options from the act of judging them; (2) broaden the options on the table rather than look for a single answer; (3) search for mutual gains; and (4) invent ways of making their decisions easy.

An additional obstacle, and perhaps a burden to this manager, can develop from being an internal part of the company. The manager will often be asked to work with individuals, established teams, and sometimes with the entire organization where conflict behavior patterns and other dispute issues may not be something the manager is aware of because of an "organizational blind spot" (Argyris, 1990). The conflict manager will possess some role power derived from his or her position with the organization. For a successful run in this type of company position, the manager's influence will rest upon his or her personal power. Leadership will not be on the basis of control but of facilitation.

Influencing the Future

Managers and leaders need to influence their employees by promoting continuous innovation and performance improvement. Some of the workforce may welcome future changes, while others are quite happy with the status quo. Driving change will be less challenging if the following strategies are adopted (Charney, 2006): (1) take a prominent role and be available to explain new initiatives; (2) challenge the people around you; (3) create strong teams with individuals who share your goals and values; (4) vary and adjust strategies to the level of urgency required; (5) embrace new ideas garnered through brainstorming techniques; and (6) communicate clearly, concisely, and constantly by holding numerous information meetings.

Several years ago, the administrative director of guidance services for a relatively large educational institution asked me to work with four members of the administration cabinet who were not cooperating well. The future of the institution was in peril with low-performing students, high truancy rates and increasing drop-out rates. The guidance director thought that working on some team building would help. After two full days of talks and assessments with the four administrators, it became clear that the issue would not be improved with cohesiveness training. There were some problems with two of the individuals who lacked self-awareness and the other two who demonstrated a lack of any deep understanding of the institution's policies and politics. The lack of empathy and rise of negative tones among the four contributed to their non-cooperation. They did not feel any sense of responsibility for the problems and avoided working together. The answer to this dilemma was to get the administrators together to engage in honest conversations about what was not working or not productive in addressing the institution's problems. These leaders needed to have a reality check on the projected future outcomes for all the stakeholders. Several weeks of meetings in quads seemed to improve the situation.

In the first weeks of 2019, Netflix, an American media-services provider headquartered in Los Gatos, California, announced that their prices were going up. As the company continues to invest in entertainment programming, Netflix's chief executive Reed Hastings indicates that the increase in subscription prices is needed to continue to increase their profits. The organization is aware of the increased competition from Amazon, Apple, Disney and AT&T's WarnerMedia. The move by Netflix is to provide revenue to offset the $18.6 billion the company has committed to spend on future content. The company's corporate vision is to continually build their customer base and previous rate increases have had little effect on subscribers.

Dynamic Network Theory

New discoveries across the social sciences highlight "social networks" as phenomena that can influence and change lives. What gives social networks power? How do they facilitate and motivate change? How can organization leaders meld social psychology's traditional focus on individual and collective goals with organizational/management science's analyses of institutional roles? How can these approaches improve the intervention, prevention and the resolution of conflict?

Social networks can profoundly influence human behavior and most people can investigate their lives to find key individuals or groups that played powerful roles in shaping their goals, dreams, and achievements. Addressing researchers and practitioners interested in new approaches to social network analysis, James Westaby (2012) postulates in *Dynamic Network Theory* that this theory has implications for topics in conflict resolution, counseling, health, education, political science/international relations, and consultation. Central to the idea about dynamic network theory is that people's networks motivate them toward goal influence and goal achievement.

Organization leaders who are tasked with managing conflicts will recognize that employees can be categorized into two groups: goal strivers and system supporters. Goal strivers are individuals that are directly trying to pursue specific goals and behaviors. These often form the issues and sub-issues in negotiation, mediation or conflict resolution discussions. System supporters are those individuals that support others in their goal pursuits. These are often team members who align with the strivers in conflicts and may complicate conflict sessions by interceding or interrupting the resolution process. On the other side are goal preventers and supportive resistors. Goal preventers are people who will attempt to prevent or thwart goal pursuits and supportive resistors support these individuals in their resistance efforts.

In organizational settings, team managers need to grasp the idea that dynamic network theory conceptualizes that groups and teams of employees represent social structures with identifiable collective goals and precise group boundaries. Many of these groups progress through a series of entrepreneurial stages (Quinn & Cameron, 1983) very similar to Tuckman's classic model. Successful company managers may recognize these stages and visualize how they play into the creation and escalation of conflict. These stages are (1) innovation (creativity and resource generation); (2) collectivity (focus on human and interpersonal relations); (3) formalization (stability and work efficiency); and (4) elaboration (structuring and monitoring the external environment.)

This theory also has implications for managers to understand the cohesion and conflict among workforce groups. This is an important area of inquiry because group cohesion has been aligned with team-level performance. With a greater understanding of this network theory, managers can see that the strength of relational coordination ties among participants in a work process can forecast outcomes that are critically and strategically important in organizations. These outcomes include quality, efficiency, customer engagement, workforce resilience and well-being, learning and innovation. Employees come to see their work differently and begin to have more productive conversations with each other that can contribute to the absence of conflicts or lessen their severity.

Barriers to the success of networked teams and individuals may be caused by the inflexibility of the corporate structure or tradition. Organization rules and regulations can cause delays and difficulties for work teams and departments. Developing and maintaining a network of contacts in senior management can help smooth out difficulties in moving to decisions and action. The higher people move in an organization, the wider the view. Top managers can collaborate across the hierarchy and connect various company networks to progress and achieve success. It is common for larger organizations to calculate senior management positions by their scope, responsibility and budgetary authority and then to assign a level to these positions. The senior manager can offer the opportunity for supervisory managers to take on new responsibilities and increase their contributions.

Imperatives for Effective Managers

The effective conflict manager ensures that employees, teams and work departments have stability over time and that they are provided with ample support and resources to complete the jobs, projects and tasks at hand. An imperative is to move quickly and decisively when opportunities for action open, without trying to foster or force interventions when the time is not right.

Group Design Shapes Group Performance

Compelling Direction	*Enabling a Group*	*Support Context*	*Group Performance*
Energizes +	Group Task Design +	Reward System =	Effort
Orients Attention +	Norms of Conduct +	Information System =	Performance Strategy
Engages Talent +	Group Composition +	Educational System =	Knowledge and Skill

Effective managers need not rely on any single strategy for promoting work team effectiveness or build the level of effort that employees apply to their work. They increase the task appropriateness of the performance strategies and help employees avoid disputes and conflicts by directing them to utilize their pool of knowledge and skills. Supportive organizational context levels the path to group excellence (Hackman, 2002).

When managers take the time to get to know employees better, they can find out what their key motivators are and what they really value in their job. For the sake of overall performance and productivity, it is imperative to resolve such conflict situations quickly and effectively before they spiral out of control.

Finally, without a doubt, running an organization is serious business. Products and services must be sold and delivered, and money must be made. Despite the gravity of these responsibilities, successful managers make their organizations exciting places to work. Having employees who enjoy coming to work, work hard, and can resolve conflict issues end up being a more loyal and energized workforce.

Case Studies

The following case studies present opportunities for individuals or small groups to practice the skills of conflict resolution, negotiation, mediation, and problem-solving. These communicative situations allow the participants to share their views and opinions with other participants. It is a systematic exchange of information, views and opinions about a topic, problem, issue or situation. These case studies can be worked on in any order and the exchange of information will present participants with new ideas. Adapting the materials in the book to these discussions is helpful; however, they can open additional avenues about many aspects of the topics covered. These case study discussions offer opportunities to improve yourself and to help identify shortcomings, weaknesses and strengths.

One technique for adapting these case studies is the fish bowl activity. The basic idea is that rather than a large group having an open discussion about some of these cases, which can be difficult to handle and often only benefits a few active participants, a smaller group (ideally two to four people) is isolated to discuss while the rest of the participants (maximum of 12 people) sit around the outside and observe without interrupting. Facilitation is focused on the core group discussion.

Although largely self-organizing once the discussion gets underway, the fishbowl process usually has a facilitator or moderator.

Case Study 1—Noisy Neighbors

Neighbor in Apartment 3A

You are the leader of your class group and you are going to make an important presentation early in the morning. It is quite late. You have prepared fully and you go to bed. But you can't sleep because the noisy neighbors are disturbing the peace again. Their loud music pounds through your walls.

The yelling and laughing is sure to keep you awake—and insomnia is hardly the ideal preparation for an important meeting in the morning.

You have had some minor arguments with these neighbors before; in fact, their daughter often babysits for you and is quite competent. You have only lived in this building for 10 months and don't know too many other neighbors. You really don't want to call the cops, so how do you resolve the noise problem and get to sleep? You decide to go over there and talk with them.

....

Neighbor in Apartment 3B

You live next door to a neighbor that is always complaining about any little thing. Yesterday, your son returned home from two tours in Iraq and you are throwing a loud and joyous welcome home/celebration party for 12 family members and close friends.

You know it's late, but this is a real occasion to bring everyone together. You don't dislike your neighbor; in fact, your daughter often babysits for her. You have lived in this building for 10 years and are good friends with almost everyone. You really don't want your neighbor to call the police, so how will you resolve the noise problem? Your neighbor is now at your door.

....

Case Study 2—Apple Bashing

On March 15, 2013, International Consumers' Day in China, the nation's largest state-run television network criticized Apple for giving iPhone customers in China a short warranty and for charging consumers to replace faulty back covers on iPhones. Apple products are immensely popular in China.

Other state media outlets joined in the Apple bashing, and the public outcry grew. Some speculated that the complaints were a calculated campaign by the Chinese governments to boost Apple's Chinese competitors.

Apple initially failed to respond to the accusations against its warranty policies. Then, in an open letter released in Chinese, CEO Timothy Cook admitted that his company's lack of communication had led to the perception that "Apple is arrogant and doesn't care or value consumers' feedback." The letter continued, "We sincerely apologize for any concern or misunderstanding this has brought to the customers."

In collectivist cultures such as Japan and China, an apology can be an especially effective means of alleviating conflict in international negotiation, regardless of whether the apologizer is to blame.

Is a company apology sufficient to resolve a conflict issue? What role does forgiveness play in this situation? Does a carefully delivered apology restore dignity and trust in a way that sheer financial compensation cannot?

Case Study 3—We Deliver

Alex is the foreman at the Move Right delivery service. He has been working there for 15 years and is a burly, no-nonsense supervisor with a proven track record of on-time deliveries with only two insurance claims over the course of his tenure.

Felipe is the vice-president of the furniture and accessories staging company Pleasant Homes. His biggest contracts involve successful television rehab people, who restore and resell properties. Felipe originally worked as a home staging specialist and now has been promoted to VP. He is often indecisive about the types of furniture, rugs, and accessories he wants to move into homes pre-sale.

Alex and Felipe have contrasting styles, but each company relies on their six-year business partnership.

Often simple delivery change requests by Felipe drive Alex nuts. How can they sit down to resolve their differences and come to a resolution that keeps Move Right and Pleasant Homes working together?

Case Study 4—Working in HR

A team of eight administrators worked in the human resources department. It was essential that they all worked as a team as their case work depended on the cooperation of each member and on all team members being up to date on developments in the company and changes in policies. Daphne joined the team about four months ago. The rest of the team members had worked together for two to four years. The team leader had also previously been a member of the team and was promoted to team leader about 10 months ago. She had been involved in the recruitment of Daphne but had been surprised at how quickly Daphne was becoming acquainted with the work and how the rest of the team looked to her for assistance. Daphne noticed that the team leader was excluding her from updates and information which she then had to rely on her colleagues to receive. There were also a couple of occasions when she was informed by colleagues outside of the department that her information was not up to date. Daphne was also excluded from several social functions. She dreaded coming to work. She felt she would have to discuss this with the team leader. She found it difficult to raise the issue directly with her and decided to find out about the mediation process.

The team leader reluctantly agreed to mediation as she initially denied that there was a problem. During mediation both individuals were encouraged to communicate on the identified issues to promote mutual understanding and to refocus on the future instead of dwelling on the current problems.

What issues came out in the initial meeting? What were the team leader's feelings toward Daphne? Why? What outcomes and resolutions could be agreed to?

Case Study 5—The Team Project

Two members of a public relations department of a medium-sized organization have been assigned to work on a presentation project. Adrien, who was an art major in college, has chosen to prepare the visuals for the project and Stacey has been left to do most of the research and writing. She believes this task is more onerous than Adrien's, and each time she tries to bring this up, Adrien brushes her off, stating that the work load is quite fair. The other three members of this project have refused to step into this dispute. It is obvious that Adrien and Stacey cannot negotiate an amicable solution.

When referred to mediation, what would the beginning, middle and end phases look like? Are there issues of leverage and power at hand here? If so, how will they be addressed? It is unclear if there is a project manager or leader in this scenario. What role does that person play?

Case Study 6—New Boss, New Rules

Your division just lost your supervisor who retired. A new supervisor has been appointed. Leland has been hired from outside the company and your team is concerned that the roles, norms, and leadership may change drastically. Leland has called for a meeting of the division and after a presentation has opened the floor for questions and concerns.

Will questions and concerns be forthcoming? What are some of the key questions that will be asked? What are some of the indirect questions that will be posed? Will the openness of the questions be the cause of problems? What would the nature of those questions be and what issues might they raise? Will politeness prevail, or will some individuals be threatened by this change and be less than supportive? Will individual(s) who felt that they should have been promoted to this position from within the company be rebellious? How will the *internal rationalizing process* affect this initial meeting: people's sense of self, attitudes toward work, past experiences, gender, age, prior relationships and conflict styles?

Case Study 7—You're Under Arrest

Within a working team it would be ideal if we could be empowered to identify areas of potential trouble that might arise. One could identify what the troublesome area is and issue an "arrest warrant" to catch and stop this behavior. A word of caution: some team members might be sensitive to this activity and become defensive, so it is best to keep this lighthearted. It is best to use this case study with individuals who trust each other.

Name of Team Member _____

Arresting Team Member _____

Place a mark next to each offense.

- { } Too competitive in most situations.
- { } Usually an avoider in decision-making.
- { } Always needing approval for actions.
- { } Brings up the past at every chance.
- { } Constantly complains about the project or work load.
- { } Views others as the foundation of his/her problems.

{ } Strong-willed and looking to sway and change others.
{ } Reticent and not very involved in the team's work.
{ } Boisterous without letting others have a chance to contribute.
{ } Highly critical of others; always throwing darts to deflate others.
{ } Quick to grab leadership and/or spotlight role.

Case Study 8—The Melt—Hops and Wine Stop—Taki-Slow

This is a negotiation involving representatives of three retail businesses: a sandwich melt-down restaurant, a local microbrewery and wine establishment, and a Chinese-Thai take-out place. The major issues are working out the details regarding a joint market space that will house each of the establishments in Culver City, California. The three businesses will need to discuss the following:

1. Each store design.
2. Common outdoor facilities that would include benches, tables and small fountains.
3. Roof-protection area with plantings.
4. Distribution of rental costs.
5. Distribution of fees paid to Culver City for outdoor eating space.
6. Purchase or rental of propane heating lamps/fans.

Case Study 9—Hawaii Beachwear Project

The CEO of Hawaii Beachwear has formed a project team to create an online knowledge-sharing system for the company website. The IT manager needs the input of one of the employees in the sales division to lead the steering committee of this team. This manager approaches the director of sales to request Ralphie Charles, one of the most successful sales people in the company, to head up the team. The director of sales might be reluctant to release Ralphie.

As the company HR negotiator, you have been asked to meet with the PM and the director. You will need to work out a collaborative agreement between the two individuals and develop a report for the CEO. Issues to be resolved include the following:

1. Viability of this project.
2. Amount of time that Ralphie will devote, if any.
3. Alternatives to releasing this sales person to the project team.

Case Study 10—Oh, What a Feeling

Identify the content, emotions and possible areas of conflict that are contained in these scenarios.

Harvey is a structural architect who has just been promoted to supervisor in his department. His promotion was a result of his superb design skills. In discussing his promotion with his manager, Rhonda, he stated, "I am looking forward to this new position, but my major concern is that I have never supervised anyone before. How can I motivate my direct reports and be an effective role model and leader?"

Content—
Emotions—
Possible conflict(s)—

Akeem is quite upset with Ramon. He has mentioned several times that Ramon "stabs me in the back all the time. He is so passive-aggressive. I find it impossible to be direct with him, and when I try to be direct, he goes behind my back to get even with me." Akeem has been working in the same department as Ramon for the last four years and was recently denied a promotion that he thought was a sure thing. He believes that Ramon's persistent negative comments were partly responsible for this.

Content—
Emotions—
Possible conflict(s)—

References

Acuff, F. (2008). *Show Me the Money.* Olympia Fields, IL: Management Development International.

Allen T., & L. Finkelstein (2003). Beyond Mentoring: Alternative Sources and Functions of Developmental Support. *Career Development Quarterly* 51, 346–355.

American Arbitration Association (2005). *Model Standards of Conduct for Mediators.* September.

Argyris, C. (1990). *Overcoming Organizational Defenses.* Englewood Cliffs, NJ: Prentice Hall.

Azzarello, P. (2012). *Rise: 3 Practical Steps for Advancing Your Career, Standing Out as a Leader, and Liking Your Life.* New York: Ten Speed Press.

Bacal, R. (1998). *Conflict Prevention in the Workplace: Using Cooperative Communication.* Winnipeg: Bacal & Associates.

Bardi, A., & Schwartz, S. H. (2003). Values and Behavior: Strength and Structure of Relations. *Personality & Social Psychology Bulletin*, October, 1208.

Barnard, C. I. (1968). *The Functions of the Executive.* Cambridge: Harvard University Press.

Barrows, H. (1980). *Problem-Based Learning: An Approach to Medical Education.* New York: Springer.

Bass, B. (1985). *Transformational Leadership.* Mahwah, NJ: Lawrence Erlbaum.

Beamer, L., & Varner, I. (2008). *Intercultural Communication in the Global Workplace.* Boston: McGraw-Hill Irwin.

Beauchamp, T. L., & Bowie, N. E. (1988). *Ethical Theory and Business, 3rd Edition.* Englewood Cliffs, NJ: Prentice Hall.

Beckhard, R. (1969). *Organization Development: Strategies and Models.* Reading, MA: Addison-Wesley.

Bednarz, T. (2011). *Effective Questioning Technique: Pinpoint Customer Service Development Training Series.* Stevens Point, WI: Majorium Business Press.

Belak, T. (1998). Intergroup Conflict in the Workplace. *Mediate.com.* Eugene, OR.

Benner, K., Kang, C., & Wakabayashi, D. (2018). In Shake-Up, Top Lobbyist for Google Steps Down. *The New York Times* (November 3), B3.

Bielenberg, J., Burn, M., Galle, G., & Dickinson, E. E. (2016). *Think Wrong: How to Conquer the Status Quo and Do Work That Matters.* San Francisco: Instigator Press.

Billing-Yun, M. (2010). *Beyond Dealmaking.* San Francisco: Jossey-Bass.

Blake R. R., & Moulton, J.S. (1964). *The Managerial Grid.* Houston: Gulf Publishing.

Blewiit, J. (1999). Problem-Based Learning. In *Human Resource Development: Learning & Training for Individuals & Organizations, 2nd Edition.* Wilson, J. P. London: Kogan Page.

Brewer, E. (2013). Managing the Ethical Implications of the Big Box: The Walmart Effect. In *Case Studies in Organizational Communication: Ethical Perspectives and Practices, 2nd Edition.* May, S. Los Angeles: Sage.

Briggs, K., & Meyers, I. B. (1943). *Meyers-Briggs Type Indicator.* Palo Alto, CA: Consulting Psychologists Press.

Brown, M. (1989). Ethics in Organizations. Markkula Center for Applied Ethics. *Ethics Magazine* 2(1).

Bryman, A. (1992). *Charisma and Leadership in Organizations.* London: Sage.

Bucaro, F. (2016). *The Trust Puzzle: How to Keep Your Company on the Ethical High Road.* Chicago: Networlding Publishing.

Burke, W. W. (2011). *Organization Change: Theory and Practice, 3rd Edition.* Los Angeles: Sage.

References

Burley-Allen, *Listening: The Forgotten Skill: A Self-Teaching Guide, 2nd Edition*. New York: John Wiley & Sons.

Cahn, D. D., & Abigail, R. (2014). *Managing Conflict Through Communication, 5th Edition*. Boston: Pearson.

Carlson, D. S., & Perrewe, P. I. (1995). Institutionalization of Organizational Ethics Through Transformational Leadership. *Journal of Business Ethics* 14(10), 828–838.

Cartwright, S., & Cooper, C. L. (1993). The Role of Culture Compatibility in Successful Organizational marriage. *Academy of Management Executive* 7(2), 62.

Casselman, B. (2018). The Power of Hungry Employees. *The New York Times* (June 26), B1, 1.

Cattell, A. (2005). Intellectual Capital. In *Human Resource Development: Learning and Training for Individuals and Organizations, 2nd Edition*. Wilson, J. London: Kogan Page.

Charney, C. (2006). *The Leader's Tool Kit*. New York: AMACOM.

Chua, R. (2013). The Costs of Ambient Cultural Disharmony: Indirect Intercultural Conflicts in Social Environment Undermine Creativity. *Academy of Management Journal* 56(6).

Cohen, H. (1980). *You Can Negotiate Anything*. New York: Bantam Books.

Conger, J. A (1999). Charismatic and Transformational Leadership in Organizations. *Leadership Quarterly* 10(2), 145–179.

Coombs, W. T. (2012). *Ongoing Crisis Management: Planning, Managing and Responding, 3rd Edition*. Thousand Oaks, CA: Sage.

Coser, L. A. (1956). *The Function of Social Conflict*. London: Routledge.

Covey, S. R. (2003). *The 7 Habits of Highly Effective People: Personal Workbook*. New York: Simon & Schuster.

CPP, Inc. (2008). Workplace Conflict: How Businesses Can Harvest it to Thrive Human Capital Report Mountain View, CA: CPP.

Dana, D. (2001) *Conflict Resolution*. New York: McGraw-Hill.

Daniels, S., & Walker, G. (2001). *Working Through Environmental Conflict: The Collaborative Learning Approach*. Westport, CT: Praeger.

De Bono, E. (1985). *Six Thinking Hats*. New York: Back Bay Books.

Deutsch, M. (1969). Conflicts: Productive and Destructive. *Journal of Social Issues* 25 (1), 7–42.

Deutsch, M. (1973). *The Resolution of Conflict: Constructive and Destructive Processes*. New Haven: Yale University Press.

Deutsch, M., & Coleman, P. (2000). *The Handbook of Conflict Resolution: Theory and Practice*. San Francisco: Jossey-Bass.

DeVito, J. (2019). *The Interpersonal Communication Book*. New York: Pearson Education.

Diamond, S. (2010). *Getting More: How to Negotiate to Achieve Your Goals in the Real World*. New York: Three Rivers Press.

Dryer, W. (1995). *Team Building: Current Issues and New Alternatives*. Reading, MA: Addison-Wesley.

Emerson, R. M. (1962). Power-Dependence Relations. *American Sociological Review* 24, 31–41.

Facione, P., & Gittens C. (2013). *Think Critically*. Boston: Pearson Education.

Feigenbaum, E. (2008). Organizational Conflict Theory. *Cron.com*. Hearst Newspapers.

Filley, A. (1975). *Interpersonal Conflict Resolution*. Glenview, IL: Scott, Foresman.

Fischer, L. (1962). *The Essential Gandhi*. New York: Vintage, 255.

Fisher, B. A. (1971). Communication Research and the Task-Oriented Group. *Journal of Communication* 21, 136–149.

Fisher, R., & Brown, S. (1988). *Getting Together: Building Relationships as We Negotiate*. New York: Penguin Books.

Folger, J., Poole, M., & Stutman, R. (2013). *Working Through Conflict: Strategies for Relationships, Groups and Organizations, 7th Edition*. Boston: Pearson.

Forsyth, D. (1999). *Group Dynamics, 3rd Edition*. Belmont, CA: Thompson.

French, J., & Raven, B. (1959). The Basis of Social Power. In *Group Dynamics*. Cartwright, D., & Zander, A. New York: Harper & Row.

Frey, R. (2015). Millennials Surpass Gen Xers as the Largest Generation in the U.S. Labor Force. *Pew Research Center*, May 11.

Fullan, M. (1991). *The New Meaning of Educational Change, 2nd Edition*. New York: Teachers College Press.

Gavin, D. (1993). Building a Learning Organization. *Harvard Business Review* (July-August).

Gitomer, J. (2011). *Jeffrey Gitomer's Little Book of Leadership: The 12.5 Strengths of Responsible, Reliable, Remarkable Leaders That Create Results, Rewards, and Resilience*. Hoboken: John Wiley & Sons.

Goleman, D. (1995). *Emotional Intelligence*. New York: Bantam Books.

Gottlieb, M., & Healy, W. J. (1998). *Making Deals: The Business of Negotiating, 2nd Edition*. Albuquerque: The Communication Project.

Griffith, D., & Goodwin, C. (2016). *Conflict Survival Kit: Tools for Resolving Conflict at Work, 2nd Edition*. Boston: Pearson.

Guillard, B., et al. (2010). Organizational Assimilation: A Multi-Dimensional Reconceptualization and Measure. *Management Communication Quarterly* 24(4), 552–578.

Hackman, R. (1987). The Design of Work Teams. In *Handbook of Organizational Behavior*. Lorsh, J. 315–342. Englewood Cliffs, NJ: Prentice Hall.

Hackman, R. J. (2002). *Leading Teams: Setting the Stage for Great Performances*. Boston: Harvard Business School Press.

Hall, E. T., & Hall, M. (1990). *Understanding Cultural Differences: Germans, French and Americans*. Boston: Nicholas Brealey Publishing.

Hall, J. (2009). To Achieve or Not: The Manager's Choice. *California Management Review* 18(4–5).

Hanson, P., & Lubin, B. (1989). Answers to Questions Frequently Asked About Organizational Development. In *The Emerging Practice of Organizational Development*. Sikes, E., Drexle, A., & Grant, J. Alexandria, VA: NTL Institute.

Hartman, A., & LeGrande, C. (2015). *Ruthless Execution: How Business Leaders Manage Through Turbulent Times*. Upper Saddle River, NJ: Pearson Education.

Harvey, J. (1988). *The Abilene Paradox and Other Meditations on Management*. New York: John Wiley.

Havelock, R. G. (1973). *The Change Agent's Guide to Innovation in Education*. Englewood Cliffs, NJ: Educational Technology Publications.

Heron, J. (1993). *Group Facilitation*. London: Kogan Page.

Hiatt, J., & Creasey, T. (2012. *Change Management: The People Side of Change*. Loveland, CO: Prosci Learning Center Publications.

International Center for Cooperation & Conflict Resolution (2009). *Collaborative Conflict Resolution*. New York: Teachers College, Columbia University.

Ivancevich, J., & Matteson, M. (2002). *Organizational Behavior and Management*. New York: McGraw-Hill.

Jackson-Cherry, L., & Bradley, E. (2010). *Crisis Intervention and Prevention*. Boston: Pearson.

Janis, I. (1972). *Victims of Groupthink*. New York: Houghton-Mifflin.

Johnson, D. W., & Johnson. F. P. (1997). *Joining Together: Group Theory and Group Skills, 6th Edition*. Boston: Allyn & Bacon.

Jones, G. (2011). *Organizational Theory, Design, and Change*. Boston: Pearson.

Kaplan, R., & Norton, D. (1992). The Balance Scorecard: Measures That Drive Performance. *Harvard Business Review* (January-February).

Kaplan, R., & Norton, D. (2004). *Strategy Mapping: Converting Intangible Assets*. Boston: Harvard Business School.

Karrass, C. L. (1993). *Give and Take: The Complete Guide to Negotiating Strategies and Tactics*. New York: Harper Business.

Kassing, J. W. (1998). Development and Validation of the Organizational Dissent Scale. *Management Communication Quarterly* 12, 183–229.

Katz, D. (1978). *The Social Psychology of Organizations*. New York: John Wiley & Sons.

Katz, D., & Kahn, R. L. (1976). *The Social Psychology of Organizations, 2nd Edition*. New York: Wiley.

Kaye, L. (2015). Five Years After Deepwater Horizon: Can BP Repair Its Reputation? *Sustainable Brands News* (February 19).

Keyton, J. (2011). *Communication and Organizational Culture: A Key to Understanding Work Experiences, 2nd Edition*. Thousand Oaks, CA: Sage.

Kilmann, R.., & Thomas, K. (1974). *Thomas Kilmann Conflict Mode Instrument*. Sunnyvale, CA: CPP.

Knapp, M. L., Vangelisti, A., & Caughlin, J. P (2014). *Interpersonal Communication and Human Relationships, 7th Edition*. Boston: Pearson.

Kolb, D., with Porter, J.L. (2015). *Negotiating at Work: Turn Small Wins into Big Gains*. New York: Wiley.

Kotter, J. P. (1996). *Leading Change*. Cambridge: Harvard Business Review Press.

Kouzes, J., & Posner, B. (1995). *The Leadership Challenge*. New York: John Wiley & Sons.

Kouzes, J., & Posner, B. (2012). *The Leadership Challenge: How to Make Extraordinary Things Happen in Organizations, 5th Edition*. San Francisco: Jossey-Bass.

Kreitner, R., & Kinicki, A. (2010). *Organizational Behavior, 9th Edition. New York: McGraw-Hill.

Kubler-Ross, E. (1969). *On Death and Dying*. New York: Scribner.

Kuhn, T. (1962). *The Structure of Scientific Revolutions, 2nd Edition*. Chicago: University of Chicago Press.

Larson, C. E., & LaFasto, F. M. J. (1989). *Teamwork: What Must Go Right/What Can Go Wrong*. Newbury Park, CA: Sage.

Latham, G., Almost, J., Mann, S., & Moore, C. (2005). New Developments in Performance Management. *Organizational Dynamics* 34 (77–87).

Lawrence, P. (1969). How to Deal with Resistance to Change. *Harvard Business Review* (January).

Lazarus, A. A. (1981). *The Practice of Multimodal Therapy*. New York: McGraw-Hill.

Lencioni, P. (2002). *The Five Dysfunctions of a Team: A Leadership Fable*. San Francisco: Jossey-Bass.

Lerner, M. D., & Shelton, R. (1999). *Comprehensive Acute Traumatic Stress Management*. Commack, NY: The American Academy of Experts in Traumatic Stress.

Levi, D., & Slem, C. (1995). Team Work in Research and Development Organizations: The Characteristics of Successful Teams. *International Journal of Industrial Ergonomics* 16, 29–42.

Levine, S. (2002). *The Book of Agreement: 10 Essential Elements for Getting the Results You Want*. San Francisco: Berrett-Koehler Publishers.

Lewicki, B., Barry, B., & Saunders, D. (2007, 2016). *Essentials of Negotiation, 6th Edition*. New York: McGraw-Hill.

Lewicki, R., Hiam, A., & Wise Olander, K. (1996). *Think Before You Speak*. New York: John Wiley & Sons.

Lewin, K. (1951). *Field Theory in Social Science*. New York: Harper & Row.

Lewis, G. (2006). *Organizational Crisis Management: The Human Factor* Boca Raton: Auerbacb Publishers.

Lindoerfer, D. (2008). Learning Mode: Adapting and Innovating is Crucial for Teams. *Leadership in Action* 28(3).

Lippitt, R., Watson, J., & Westerly, B. (1958). *The Dynamics of Planned Change*. Orlando: Harcourt Brace.

Livermore, D. (2015). *Leading with Cultural Intelligence: The Real Secret to Success*. New York: AMACOM.

Lockwood, Thomas (2009). *Design Thinking*. New York: Allworth Press/DMI.

Luft, J., & Ingham, H. (1955). The Johari Window: A Graphic Model of Interpersonal Awareness. Los Angeles: University of California Los Angeles.

Mannix, E., Neale, M., & Blount-Lyon, S. (2004). *Research in Managing Groups and Teams: Temporal Issues*. Oxford: Elsevier Science Press.

Marquis, H. (2007). Impact Assessment in 5 Easy Steps. *DITY Newsletter* (January).

Maslow, A. (1954). *Motivation and Personality*. New York: Harper & Row.

McGrath, J. (1984). *Groups: Interactions and Performance*. Englewood Cliffs, NJ: Prentice Hall.

Mehrabian, A. (1971). *Silent Messages*. Belmont, CA: Wadsworth.

Melville-Ross, T. (2013). Ethical Business: Companies Need to Earn Our Trust. *The Guardian*, July 11.

Merchant, N. (2010). *The New How: Building Business Solutions Through Collaborate Strategy*. North Sebastopol, CA: O'Reilly Media.

Messick, D. (1999). Alternative Logics for Decision Making in Social Settings. *Journal of Economic Behavior & Organization* 39(1), 11–28.

Michalko, M. (2006). *Thinkertoys: A Handbook of Creative-Thinking Techniques, 2nd Edition*. Berkeley: Ten Speed Press.

Mitchell, T. (1982). Motivation: New Directions for Theory, Research and Practice. *Academy of Management Review* 7, 80–88.

Mittleman, D., & Briggs, R. (1999). Communication Technologies for Traditional and Virtual Teams. *Supporting Work Team Effectiveness*. Sundstrom, E., 246–270. San Francisco: Jossey-Bass.

Moore, C. (1996, 2003). *The Mediation Process: Practical Strategies for Resolving Conflicts*. San Francisco: Jossey-Bass.

Morrison, T., & Conaway, W. (2006). *Kiss, Bow, or Shake Hands: The Bestselling Guide to Doing Business in More Than 60 Countries, 2nd Edition*. Avon, MA: Adams Media.

Natemeyer, W. E., & Hersey, P. (2011). *Classics of Organizational Behavior, 4th Edition*. Long Grove, IL: Waveland Press.

Nesbett, R., & Ross, L. (1980). *Human Inferences: Strategies and Shortcomings of Social Judgment*. Englewood Cliffs, NJ: Prentice Hall.

Noe, R. 2002. *Employee Training and Development, 2nd Edition*. New York: McGraw-Hill Irwin.

References

Noe, R., Hollenbeck, J., Gerhart, B., & Wright, P. (2010), *Human Resource Management: Gaining a Competitive Edge, 7th Edition*. New York: McGraw-Hill Irwin.

Nosseir, M. (2016). The Collaboration vs. Competition Dilemma Among Business Executives. *Entrepreneur Middle East*, September 19.

O'Toole, I. (1995). *Leading Change: Overcoming the Ideology of Comfort and the Tyranny of Custom*. San Francisco: Jossey-Bass.

Osterman, P. (1994). How Common Is Workplace Transformation and Who Adopts It? *Industrial and Labor Relations Review* 47, 172–188.

Payne, V. (2001). *The Team-Building Workshop: A Trainer's Guide*. New York: AMACOM, 209–214.

Peltier, B. (2010). *The Psychology of Executive Coaching: Theory and Application, 2nd Edition*. New York: Routledge.

Peters, T., & Waterman, R. (1982). *In Search of Excellence*. New York: HarperCollins.

Pfeffer, J. (1992). *Managing with Power: Politics and Influence in Organizations*. Cambridge: Harvard Business School.

Pink, D. H. (2011). *Drive: The Surprising Truth About What Motivates Us*. New York: Riverhead Books.

Porath, C., & Pearson, C. (2009). *The Cost of Bad Behavior: How Incivility Is Damaging Your Business and What to Do About It*. New York: Penguin.

Porter, M. E. (1985). *Competitive Advantage: Creating and Sustaining Superior Performance*. New York: The Free Press.

Prahalad, C., & Ramaswamy, V. (2004). Co-Creation Experiences: The Next Practice in Value Creation. *Journal of Interactive Marketing* 18(3).

Psychometrics (2010). Warring Egos, Toxic Individuals, Feeble Leadership. Retrieved from http://www.psychometrics.com/docs/conflictstudy_09.pdf on May 11, 2012.

Puleo, S., & McGlothlin, J. (2010). Overview of Crisis Intervention. In *Crisis Intervention and Prevention*. Jackson-Cherry, L.R., & Erford, B. Boston: Pearson.

Quinn, R. E., & Cameron, K. (1983). Organizational Life Cycle and Shifting Criteria of Effectiveness. *Management Science* 29, 33–51.

Rahim, M. A. (2002). Toward a Theory of Managing Organizational Conflict. *The International Journal of Conflict Management* 13(3), 206–235.

Ré, E. F. (2003). *101 Secrets to Negotiating Success*. Albuquerque: Canyon Crest Publishing.

Reed, S. (2018). Swiss Commodities Giant Faces U.S. Subpoena in Corruption Inquiry. *The New York Times*, July 4, B3.

Rima, S. (2000). *Leading from the Inside Out: The Art of Self-Leadership*. Grand Rapids: Baker Book House Company.

Robbins, S., & Judge, T. A. (2018). *Essentials of Organizational Behavior, 14th Edition*. Harlow, England: Pearson.

Robertson, P., Roberts, D., & Porras, J. (1993). Dynamics of Planned Organizational Change: Assessing Empirical Support for a Theoretical Model. *Academy of Management Journal* 36(3), 619–634.

Saba, T. (2013). Understanding Generational Differences in the Workplace: Findings and Conclusions. *Industrial Relations Center, Queens University*. Kingston, Ontario.

Salancik, G. R., & Pfeffer, J. (2011). Who Gets Power—and How They Hold on to It. In *Classics of Organizational Behavior, 4th Edition*. Natemeyer, W., & Hersey, P. Long Grove, IL: Waveland Press.

Savin-Baden, M (2003). *Facilitating Problem-Based Learning: Illuminating Perspectives*. Buckingham: Open University Press.

Scandura, T. (2019). *Essentials of Organizational Behavior: An Evidence-Based Approach*. Los Angeles: Sage.

Schellenberg, J. (1996). *Conflict Resolution: Theory, Research, and Practice*. Albany: SUNY Press.

Schmidt, W.H., & Tannenbaum, R. (1960). Management of Differences *Harvard Business Review* (November).

Schneider, W. (2017). *Lead Right for Your Company's Type*. New York: AMACOM.

Schwartz, H., & Davis, S. (1981). Matching Corporate Culture and Business Strategy. *Organizational Dynamics*, 30–48.

Senge, P. (2006). *The Fifth Discipline: The Art & Practice of the Learning Organization*. New York: Currency Doubleday.

Shaw, M.E (1981). *Group Dynamics: The Psychology of Small Group Behavior*. New York: McGraw-Hill.

Shell, G. R. (2006). *Bargaining for Advantage: Negotiation Strategies for Reasonable People*. New York: Penguin.

Silberman, M. (2006). *Active Training: A Handbook of Techniques, Designs, Case Examples, and Tips*. San Francisco: Pfeiffer.

References

Simkin, W. (1971). *Mediation and the Dynamics of Collective Bargaining.* Washington, D.C.: Bureau of National Affairs.

Slaikeu, K. A. (1990). *Crisis Intervention: A Handbook for Practice and Research,* 2nd edition. Boston: Allyn & Bacon.

Society for Human Resource Management (2018). *Managing Difficult Employees and Disruptive Behaviors.* March 30, 2018.

Stayer, R. (1990). How I Learned to Let My Workers Lead. *Harvard Business Review* (November-December).

Stewart. T. (2001). *The Wealth of Knowledge: Intellectual Capital and the Twenty-First Century Organization.* New York: Doubleday.

Stone, D., Patton, B., & Heen, S. (2010). *Difficult Conversations: How to Discuss What Matters Most.* New York: Penguin Books.

Su, H. (2014). Business Ethics and the Development of Intellectual Capital. *Journal of Business Ethics* 119(1), 87–93.

Sundstrom, E., DeMeuse, K., & Futrell, D. (1990). Work Teams. *American Psychologist* 45, 120+.

Sutton, R. (2007). *The No Asshole Rule: Building a Civilized Workplace and Surviving One That Isn't.* New York: Warner Business Books.

Szalai, I., & Wessel, J. D. (2018). The Widespread Use of Workplace Arbitration Among America's Top 100 Companies. *The Employee's Rights Advocacy Institute for Law and Policy* (March, 1–12, A1-A11).

Tannenbaum, R., & Massarik, F. (1957). Leadership: A Frame of Reference. *Management Science* 4 (1).

Tapscott, D. (2009). *Grown Up Digital: How the Net Generation Is Changing Your World.* New York: McGraw-Hill.

Taylor F. W. 1912 (1984). *Scientific Management.* New York: Harper & Brothers.

Thiel, P., & Masters, B. (2015). *Zero to One: Notes on Startups, Or How to Build the Future.* New York: Crown.

Thompson, L., Peterson, E., & Brodt, S. E. (1996). "Team Negotiation: An Examination of Integrative and Distributive Bargaining." *Journal of Personality and Social Psychology*, 70(1), 66–78.

Tjosvold, D. (1993). *Learning to Manage Conflict: Getting People to Work Together Productively.* New York: Lexington Books.

Truskie, S. (2010). *Leadership in High Performance Organizational Culture,* 2nd Edition. Pittsburgh: MSD Leadership Consultants.

Tuckman, B. (1965). Developmental Sequence in Small Groups. *Psychological Bulletin* 63(6), 384–399.

United States Bureau of Labor Statistics (2016). "Number of Fatal Work Injuries."

Ury, W., Fisher, R., & Patton, B. (2011). *Getting to Yes: Negotiating Agreement Without Giving In.* New York: Penguin.

Volkema, R. (1999). *The Negotiation Tool Kit: How to Get Exactly What You Want in Any Business or Personal Situation.* New York: AMACOM.

Voss, C. (2016). *Never Split the Difference: Negotiating as if Your Life Depended on It.* New York: Harper Business.

Waldorn, V. R., & Kassing, J. W. (2011). *Managing RISK in Communication Encounters: Strategies for the Workplace.* Thousand Oaks, CA: Sage.

Wall, J. (1985). *Negotiation: Theory and Practice.* Glenview, IL: Scott Foresman.

Watson, Carol (1996). Managers as Negotiators: A Test of Power versus Gender as Predictors of Feelings, Behavior and Outcomes. *The Leadership Quarterly* 7(1), 63–85.

Weber, M. (1947). *The Theory of Social and Economic Organizations.* New York: Oxford University Press.

West, R., & Turner, L. (2000). *Introducing Communication Theory: Analysis and Application.* Mountainview, CA: Mayfield.

West Milford Center (2018). *Generational Differences Chart.* Shepherd, MO.

Westaby, J. D. (2012). *Dynamic Network Theory: How Social Networks Influence Goal Pursuit.* Washington, D.C.: American Psychological Association.

Wheatley, M. (2006). *Leadership from the New Sciences: Discovering Order in a Chaotic World.* Oakland: Berrett-Koehler.

Wheelan, S. A. (2013). *Creating Effective Teams: A Guide for Members and Leaders,* 4th Edition. Los Angeles: Sage.

Wood. J. T. (2010). *Gendered Lives: Communication, Gender and Culture,* 9th edition. Belmont, CA: Wadworth.

Zaleznik, A. (1970). Power and Politics in Organizational Life. *Harvard Business Review*, May.

Zaleznik, A. (1977). Managers and Leaders: Are They Different? *Harvard Business Review* 55(3), 67–68.

Zander, A. (1950). Resistance to Change: Its Analysis and Prevention. *Advanced Management Journal.*

Index

Abilene Paradox 108–109, 217
active listening 159–161
agents of change 200
Albert Mehrabian 7/38/5 Rule 163
antecedents of conflict 39–40
arbitration 172–174; advantages and disadvantages 173
art of seeking peace 187
assertive confrontational communication 187–188
assimilation process 69
ATP Manufacturing 13

BASICS model of the crisis experience 119
Billboard Magazine 59
British Petroleum Exploration & Production 115
building rapport 159

change management 2, 52, 82; phases 82
change model 49
Chinese symbol for crisis 9
classical organization theory 18
climate of resistance 53
cognitive development: growth 15; theory 15
collaboration: advantages 124; ineffective 133
common ground 34, 43, 52, 91, 137, 152–153, 190, 197
communication profile styles 102
conflict: intergroup 19; interpersonal 27; management personalities 100; manager 190–191, 193, 195 196, 199, 201, 204; problematic situations 36
cooperation and competition 80
crisis: essential elements 115; management plan 116, 120, 121; management team 120
critical thinking 198
cross-cultural leadership 33
cultural awareness 33
cultural differences 30; disharmony 32
cultural friction 33
cultural orientation 30
cultural patterns in organization 22

data, relationship and structural conflicts 44
de Bono, Edward *see* Six Thinking Hats
deindividuation impact 138
design thinking 175–176
differences among workers, managers and leaders 63
downward communication 65
dynamic of trust 28
dysfunctional organization 55
dysfunctional view of organizational conflict 38

effective organizational development 24
effective questioning 157
empathic responses 161
employee training 48, 219
establishing trust 29
ethics: behavior 164; leader standards 97; moral issues 95
eustress to distress 83

facilitation skills 85, 197
fight/flight response 180
fish bowl activity 207
Flint water crisis 133
forming, storming, norming, and performing 66

gender or power 32
generational differences chart 110
goal strivers and system supporters 203
ground rules 14, 17
group: characteristics 123–125; roles 20; successes 127–128
groupthink symptoms 108

healthy conflict 27
hostile work environment 32
human needs 39
human resource concerns 23

I-statements 179
imbalance of power 28
impediments to active listening 161
information exchange 148

221

investments in training and automation 14
issues, positions and interests 152

Johari Window 90, 91
John Kotter change model 49
Johnson & Johnson's Tylenol 5
Johnsonville Sausage 68

Kraft Foods Inc. 11

language of conflict 43
lateral communication 65
lateral thinking 140
leaders and managers 50, 60–61, 193; attribution error 62
leading change *see* John Kotter change model
learning organizations 10, 12–13
leveling the playing field 196
leverage 74–75

maintenance roles 20
management: ground rules 14; styles and assumptions 192; toolbox essentials 195
maturity and immaturity theories 19
McDonald's 116
mediation phase characteristics 170
mediators 169
mindset guidelines 113
model of planned change 88
motivations for working 104
Myers-Briggs Type Indicator 21

negotiation: collaborative 147; competitive 149; distributive 147, framing 155–156; objectives 150; pitfalls, ploys, and tactics 165; principled 10; principles of 152; roadblocks 166; strategies 148–149; teams 154
non-listening behaviors 159
nonverbal communication elements 162–163

occupational stress 82
open manager characteristics 191
Organizational Assimilation Index 70
organizational behavior 2, 18, 25–26, 192
organizational conflict 38
organizational development theory 89
organizational 360 assessment 184–185

paradigm shift 86
performance appraisals 41
Phi-Services, LLC 137
Piaget, Jean *see* cognitive development growth

politics and power 80
power and influence 71–73
problem-based learning 15–16

question, quiz and quantify 176

relationship violence 118
resistance to change 52–54, 83–84, 88
return-on-investment 163
role models 98

Schultz, Howard *see* Starbucks
self-awareness and self-esteem 90
Six Thinking Hats 139–141, 216
small groups developmental sequence 66
social exchange theory 41
Starbucks 5–6, 11–12, 58
Starbucks and Seattle's Best *see* Kraft Foods, Inc
strategic management planning 57
strategy mapping 64
stress management questionnaire 86
stressors 83
successful groups development 127

team: building 130; collaboration benefits 134; learning 16–17
Tesla, Inc. 26
Thomas-Kilmann Instrument 44–45
training and development programs 48
transformational leadership 58–60
Transformational Leadership Theory 59
transformative motivation agendas 103
transitions to change 85
turf battles 135

unbalanced organizational culture 22
unmotivated employees 104
upward communication 65

value: of assets 99; conflict resolution 144; personality and chance 192
virtual information technology 138
virtual teams 137–138

Walmart 96
win-win resolutions 201
workforce motivations 103
workforce resistance 54
workplace: communication 65, 178; conflict 46; morale 182; social support 29; violence policies 118

Printed in the USA
CPSIA information can be obtained
at www.ICGtesting.com
CBHW020815061223
2353CB00023B/97

9 781476 678924